Visible Learning

Day by Day

Hands-on Teaching Tools Proven
to Increase Student Achievement

Felicia Durden, Ed.D.

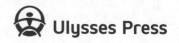
Ulysses Press

Published in the United States by:
Ulysses Press
P.O. Box 3440
Berkeley, CA 94703
www.ulyssespress.com

ISBN: 978-1-61243-765-1
Library of Congress Control Number: 2017952137

Printed in Canada by Marquis Book Printing
10 9 8 7 6 5 4 3 2 1

Acquisitions editor: Bridget Thoreson
Managing editor: Claire Chun
Editor: Shayna Keyles
Proofreader: Renee Rutledge
Front cover design: Christopher Cote
Interior design: Jake Flaherty
Front cover artwork: road and pointers © zmicier kavabata/shutterstock.com; education icons © Happy Art/shutterstock.com
Interior artwork: All images from shutterstock.com. pencil, book, calculator, and globe © Happy Art; pointer on pages 5, 11, 22, 32, 42, 50, 72, 94, 116, 131, 147, 167 © zmicier kavabata; pages 51, 112 © Torwaistudio; page 55 © Lucky clover; page 59 © mythja; page 73 © Irina Strelnikova; page 82 © robuart; page 95 © studioworkstock; page 101 © Merfin; page 106 © bel_ka; page 117 © Decorwithme; page 132 © Artisticco; page 148 © NatalyaOst; page 159 © Iconic Bestiary; page 164 © Milles Vector Studio

Distributed by Publishers Group West

Contents

Chapter 5: Parent Communication and Visible Learning Research 42

Chapter 6: Implementing Visible Learning When Planning for Instruction 50

Chapter 7: Implementing Visible Learning in Your Management System. 72

Chapter 8: Implementing Visible Learning in Your Literacy Program 94

Chapter 9: Implementing Visible Learning in Your Math Program 116

Chapter 10: Implementing Visible Learning Assessment and Grading Practices 131

Chapter 11: What Doesn't Work? 147

Chapter 12: Next Steps................................... 167

Conclusion... 174

Appendix 176

Acknowledgments... 183

About the Author 185

Introduction

In this age of high stakes testing and innovation, teachers across the world are bombarded with strategies and research-based learning approaches to try in their classrooms. Everyone claims to have the solution for all our educational woes, but let me assure you: there is no cure-all in education. As my father says, if it sounds too good to be true, it is.

This book is not about doom and gloom, but about making a balanced effort to provide your students with the most highly tested and recommended methods to improve their learning. It is laid out in a workbook format so you can easily use the tools that are related to each high-leverage strategy discussed within.

I don't know about you, but I am always interested in reading the research behind the research. I listen avidly to NPR, study all the latest medical research, and am a PBS junkie. My zeal for learning has been my driver for as long as I can remember. Due to this attraction, writing this book has been an absolute joy. It has provided an opportunity to sift through John Hattie's intensive meta-analysis of thousands of research studies and provide a synthesis of this work in practical, understandable terms. However, as a teacher, you don't have the time to read through pages and pages of research. You just need to know what strategies and practices work, and how to use them with your kids. That is precisely what this book will provide for you.

How to Use this Book

This book is not intended to be a checklist to use as you instruct, nor should it be used to create a list of primary strategies to apply with your students. This was never John Hattie's intention when he completed his meta-analysis. Instead, this book should be a guide to improve on what you are already doing. We know that most of what we are doing in schools works. Each day, we provide students with a quality education. Teaching is not easy, and this book only highlights the miracle work that you do as a teacher. With support and strong pedagogy, you work with kids to produce amazing results.

I have worked in the field of education for over 20 years, and I have witnessed those lightbulb moments when a student gets it. There is no better feeling than seeing the results of your labor bloom. Use this book to reinforce the strategies that you are using that work. Additionally, use it to make decisions about things you might want to tweak or do less of to increase your level of impact. As an educator, you instinctively know when something is working and when something needs to be monitored and adjusted. That is a part of that competency that all teachers possess. Use this book to hone your instincts and help you take a balanced approach to education.

How Is This Book Organized?

This book has 12 jam-packed, resource-filled chapters of relevant information about the practices that John Hattie evaluated. Each chapter will provide a synthesis of the interventions and their effect sizes, along with practical explanations of how to implement and evaluate them in your school or school system. The book follows a workbook model, so each chapter has journaling prompts, reflective exercises, and quizzes to take. It is important that you take the time and effort to complete these tasks, as they will allow you to gain more precise knowledge about each practice and how they relate to your own teaching system.

Chapter 1 will teach you just the right amount of information about John Hattie's 800+ study meta-analysis and the implications he drew from those studies. Consider this chapter your simplified overview of what you need to know.

In Chapters 2 through 5, you'll learn about the high-impact practices and strategies that Hattie teased out of the research. We'll discuss methods to ensure teachers can implement the high-leverage instructional and systems strategies that the research supports. Chapter 2 is about growth mindset, a critical trait that teachers and students will need to embody in order to facilitate educational growth. In recent years, there has been a lot of interest in growth mindset and grit, which, as psychology teaches us, truly aids in moving students toward their academic and social goals.

Chapter 3 explores collaboration and working together as a team of professionals to discuss best practices, and how they will look in your school. Collaboration takes away the isolated methods of teaching that I experienced in the 80's, when we closed the door and taught, and opens up the practice to involve discussion and strategy sessions to improve practice.

Chapter 4 looks at teacher clarity and explores the importance of teachers having a clear understanding of their subject matter so they can present this information coherently to students. This prevents misconceptions on the part of the student.

Chapter 5 rounds out this section and focuses on parent communication. Here, we explore how parent involvement helps expand efforts to impact student growth. When we get parents more positively involved in their children's academic lives, the achievement results are substantive.

Next, we get into the specific visible learning strategies and discuss their impact on students in positive, negative, and diminutive ways. Chapter 6 focuses on planning for instruction and provides key strategies you can use to make your planning more impactful. Chapter 7 delves into management and shares the key systems and strategies that research has shown helps kids become more successful in managing their behavior.

Chapter 8 looks at literacy. We'll explore instructional practices that will provide at least one year's growth. The practices and procedures in this chapter will help you clarify what works best in literacy instruction, sift through the numerous strategies available, and pick the most promising ones. Chapter 9 looks at promising mathematics strategies that will yield a year or more of growth. We will look at systems and instructional tools that can impact math instruction.

Chapter 10 provides insights on key strategies and systems that are worthwhile in assessment and evaluation. The chapter may give you some new tools to make assessment a more interactive process between the teacher and student. You will learn ways to make assessment more student focused and find ways to use assessment to drive your instructional practices. You will also look at assessments and how they can empower your students to be more self-sufficient learners.

While chapters 2 through 10 talk about what works, in Chapter 11, we switch the focus and look at practices with minimal positive effect, as well as some that research finds do not work. This chapter will be especially important, because we talk about ways to make changes if you are currently using lower yielding strategies. It will also provide an opportunity to assess your current reality and determine what you can change and what is outside of your realm of influence.

Finally, you'll read a summary of the learning discussed throughout the book. Chapter 12 provides reflection exercises that will allow you to look at your current reality and make plans for positive change. This chapter allows you the opportunity to reflect on the research and develop an action plan that is easy to implement in your particular setting.

The book's appendix provide resources for books, websites, and organizations that can assist you as you build your instructional practices to impact student growth. This will challenge you to utilize your growth mindset and move toward collective inquiry to start the conversation that will bring sustained, incremental change.

CHAPTER 1

A Brief Overview of Visible Learning

What Is Visible Learning?

This book provides an overview of John Hattie's visible learning research. Visible learning is, as its name suggests, a way to make learning more open and more easily describable to students and teachers. The term "visible" indicates bringing a practice to light, allowing it to be examined and probed so we can understand it more. We can look at our instructional practices and determine how effective or ineffective they are. In this book, we will look at instructional practices that have been research-proven to increase student achievement, as well as practices that have been proven to negatively impact achievement.

Who Is John Hattie?

John Hattie is a researcher from the University of Melbourne, Australia, where he serves as the Director of the Melbourne Educational Research Institute. Hattie took the education world by storm with the publication of *Visible Learning for Teachers* in 2008. His research base is one of the largest studies ever conducted, with over 800 meta-studies that included over 80 million students.

Hattie's analysis provides an insight into thousands of studies and gives us a clear picture of what practices have been correlated with success. His work allows us to make inferences about the practices that extend across socioeconomic, racial, ethnic, gender, and geographic boundaries. This is truly groundbreaking, because his research indicates that there are practices that succeed across all demographics and can be tools for bridging the achievement gap.

What Is Meta-Analysis?

A meta-analysis is an analysis of the results of multiple scientific studies to determine if there is a common thread. Such analysis allows a researcher to make an assumption about the transferability of a single practice. Meta-analysis allows a researcher to look for common themes and outcomes to make a general conclusion about the effectiveness or ineffectiveness of a given strategy.

Often, researchers are criticized for the lack of diversity and the low number of research participants in a study. What makes meta-analysis so exciting is that it involves looking at multiple studies before drawing conclusions, so there is greater diversity and a much larger pool of research participants.

What Is Effect Size, and How Is It Measured?

Effect size is a statistical measurement that quantifies the difference between two groups. In other words, it is a way of measuring how two groups might respond differently to a similar treatment. The comparison can be between an experimental and control group, or even the same group before and after a treatment.

Taking an effect size measurement is especially useful when comparing groups in experiments that are not measured on familiar scales; for example, letter grades. Instead, effect size is calculated by a simple formula that makes it easy to compare the effectiveness of an intervention, while also accounting for variation within a group.

We might calculate effect size to determine how much of an effect an intervention has on a given task, like reading or math ability. In education, it helps us determine not what intervention or programs work, but which intervention and programs work best. This is important to note, as it allows us to make more strategic decisions on what we utilize in instruction to impact achievement.

Effect size is calculated by measuring the difference between groups, then dividing by the mean standard deviation. Here is the formula for finding an effect size:

[Mean of Group One (pre-assessment group or experimental group)]
− [Mean of Group Two (post-assessment group or control group)]
_____ = Effect Size
Average Standard Deviation

John Hattie's magic number is 0.40, which relates to one year's positive growth in a single academic year. He determined this is the effect size correlated with progress when moving from one year to the next.

Anything below 0.40 indicates less than a year of growth. An average effect size is 0 to 0.40, which is what the typical teacher will afford with the normal instructional strategies used in schools. Anything below zero shows a reverse effect on student growth and indicates that students will suffer negative growth. This book provides key strategies that boost students to achieve a year or more of growth in one academic year.

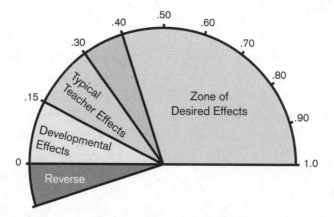

In *Visible Learning for Teachers*, Hattie talks about reverse effects, developmental effects, teacher effects, and desired effects. Reverse effects are those things that hinder or retard student growth; naturally, they have a negative effect size.

These are things like mobility (-0.34) and retention (-0.16), which will be covered more thoroughly in Chapter 11. Developmental effects, including things like gender (0.12) and diversity of students (0.05), are those things that kids experience naturally, which have little to no correlation to formal schooling. Typically, these effect sizes fall in the 0.0 to 0.15 range.

The next category is teacher effects. This refers to the average effect of common teaching practices, with effect sizes falling in the 0.20 to 0.40 range. Things like teacher verbal ability (0.22) and homework (0.29) fall in this category. Lastly, Hattie examined desired effects, which tend to have effect sizes above 0.40. This refers to practices that yield a high level of return of a year's worth of growth of more. Practices like response to intervention (1.07) and feedback (0.75) fall in this category.

Hattie's Rankings

Hattie ranked the effect sizes of the studies in his meta-analysis from 1, highest effect size, to 150, lowest effect size. These rankings show the progression of positive effect of the influences Hattie researched. At the top of the list is self-reported grading/student expectations, which had an impressive 1.44 effect size. Effect sizes of 1 and above mean that the influence is one standard deviation above the mean, which is very good. At the bottom of the list at 150 is mobility, which had an effect size of -0.034. This indicates that students decrease in their learning due to this effect.

In order for any initiative, intervention, program, or plan to produce optimal results, it must be executed with fidelity and understanding. To this point, Hattie talks about mind frames and teacher understanding. He notes that in order for schools to improve, teachers must apply growth mindset and believe that the kids can achieve, and that they, as teachers, can impart instruction that will yield high change. They must understand what they are teaching and present information to students clearly so they understand their learning expectations. Finally, Hattie is a proponent of allowing teachers to collaborate to improve in their instructional practices in order to positively impact student learning. Each of these practices—growth mindset, teacher clarity, and collaboration—will be explored in future chapters.

Doesn't Everything Work?

Most teachers have found success in the programs and strategies that they have used in their classroom. There are typically only a few students who fall behind, but for the most part, many of your students learn and move forward to the next grade level without any problem. But, let's think about that. If most everything works, why do America's schools continue to lag behind? Primary school children in the United States are falling behind children in other countries in mathematics. This trend is also being seen in our secondary schools.[1] The National Assessment of Educational Progress (NAEP), or the "Nation's Report Card," says that progress in secondary schools has stagnated in some areas while declining in others.[2] Research has continued to indicate that we are making gains in some areas, but we still have work to be done. This shows that although many of our practices are fruitful, there are some things that we need to reevaluate and possibly remove from our school systems.

In this book, you will learn about practices that may be staples in your school community, like retention, homework, and summer school, that are proven to be unfavorable for student growth. You will also learn that some things work, but maybe not as well as others, like mentoring and ability grouping. This book will help you make informed decisions about the practices you employ as you become more versed on what works best and what practices have little positive impact.

So, in short, not everything works. Some things work better than others, some practices have minimal effect, and some practices retard student growth and set kids back. Thus, taking the time to fully understand these ideas is important for your own personal growth.

---

1   A. H. Schoenfeld, Making mathematics work for all children: Issues of standards, testing, and equity, Educational Researcher 31, no. 1 (2002): 13-25.

2   NAEP, "NAEP Report Cards," The Nation's Report Card, Accessed December 5, 2017, https://www.nationsreportcard.gov.

Why Should I Care About Hattie's Study?

Hattie's research provides an important opportunity to discuss what is going on in our schools today. In the 1990s, institutions like the National Reading Panel began to perform in-depth analyses to determine best teaching practices for reading. This was groundbreaking research that changed the way we taught reading. During that time, I served as a Title I reading specialist. I relished in the research, and it was exciting to see our reading programs transform. I believe that as we become more familiar with Hattie's research, we should get on the learning end and see how it can impact our practices.

Another important reason to care about Hattie's research is that for the first time, we can substantiate which practices work and which do not. The rankings that Hattie provide can help us make better decisions about the practices we employ. I look at it like being a wise consumer: I have read *Consumer Reports* magazine for years because I want to know which product has been tried, tested, and proven to be best. This is a simplified way of looking at Hattie's rankings, but if we use this same type of thinking, we can make informed decisions that will have a greater impact on student achievement.

The final reason you should care about Hattie's research is that we are in the field of education to prepare students for the future. No teacher goes to work each day without wanting their students to achieve at high levels. This goes beyond national testing and achievement levels; at the core of our profession is a desire for our students to be successful and grow. Think about those kids you've had in your class who showed growth in reading or math and how proud and happy it made you feel. Think also about how it felt when kids came to your class and did not show much growth. Maybe you felt like you did not do enough, or that you didn't have the skills necessary to help those particular students.

Hattie's correlates will help you sift through the minutia of research and hone in on those best practices you can start using immediately to help *all* of your students grow to their greatest potential. That is why I am so excited about this book and the research I am sharing. It will help you cut through the guess work and get down to the best practices to impact learning.

CHAPTER 2

Growth Mindset and Visible Learning Research

One of the important dispositions that Hattie's research supports is a growth mindset. Growth mindset comes from research conducted by Carol Dweck. In her 2007 book *Mindset: The New Psychology of Success*, Dweck discusses the different attributes of those with growth mindset versus those with a fixed mindset.

GROWTH MINDSET	FIXED MINDSET
Believes that talent can be developed over time with support and training.	Believes that talent is set and is solely responsible for creating success. If you don't have the talent, you cannot do it.
Relishes mistakes as an opportunity to get better and grow.	Does not take on challenges; if they do, it is done in reluctance.
Thinks about how they can grow as an individual.	Wants to look smart in front of others.

Having a growth mindset allows teachers and students to view their learning as a journey. Mistakes are inevitable, and growing from those mistakes is imperative for success. As a teacher, promoting growth mindset requires that you develop strategies to help students take risks and not shy away from undertaking new learning and challenges. This can require you to shift how you address student learning and what you articulate to your students as they take on new challenges.

For example, instead of praising a student for being smart, you would praise them for thinking outside of the box and using strategies to solve a problem. I remember that when I was a teacher, I would often praise my kids without providing specific examples, which would have helped them see how they were growing as learners. This is an example of fixed mindset. When we are not specific in our praise, students have no idea where they are and thus cannot gauge how near or far they are from the targeted goal. With a fixed mindset, we often stifle student's ability to see how they are growing and performing in relation to their set goal. In the next section, we will talk about goal setting and how it relates to cultivating a growth mindset.

Goal Setting ○ Effect Size of 0.50

One way to teach kids to develop a growth mindset is to teach them about goal setting. Goal setting has a positive effect size of 0.50, which deems it a very promising practice to use with students. Of course, setting goals for just the sake of setting goals is not beneficial for student growth. When establishing goals, we want to ensure the goals are attainable and that we have a way to assess whether we have accomplished our goals.

When students and teachers set goals, it is important that the goals are SMART goals. George T. Doran's article, "There's a S.M.A.R.T. Way to Write Management's Goals and Objectives," appeared in a 1981 issue of *Management Review* and is attributed with being the first time the SMART acronym was used. They acronym stands for goals that are specific, measurable, attainable, relevant, and time-bound.

S **Specific:** Goals should be specific and state exactly what the desired outcome is.

M **Measurable:** Goals should include a measurement that will be used to measure success.

A **Attainable:** The goal should be achievable. Goals should not be so lofty that the student cannot achieve them.

R **Relevant:** Goals should be relevant to the student, and not something vague that will not impact their learning.

T **Time-Bound:** Setting a time to reassess the goal is important so students learn to monitor their progress toward accomplishing their goal.

Related to goal setting is Alfred Bandura's self-efficacy theory, which emerged in the 1970s. Self-efficacy is the belief that one can succeed in a given situation or specific area. Students that have self-efficacy often challenge themselves and take on tasks that are difficult. They don't blame others when they face challenges or fail, but are able to understand which things are in their control and which things are not.

Students as young as kindergarten age can practice goal setting with proper supervision and training. The key to establishing goal setting is to model the practice and provide opportunities for students to set goals.

✎ Reflection

How have you used goal setting in your personal life?

_____

_____

_____

Write about a time when you set a goal for yourself and accomplished it.

_____

_____

_____

What helped you be successful in accomplishing this goal?

_____

_____

_____

What are some areas that you can set goals with your students?

_____

_____

_____

How will you ensure the goals that you set with students are SMART goals?

_____

_____

_____

📖 Resource

Use these prompts to help students construct SMART goals.

S Specific: What is your specific goal?

_____

_____

_____

M Measurable: How will you measure success?

_____

_____

_____

A Attainable: What steps will you take to accomplish your goal?

_____

_____

_____

R Relevant: Why is this goal important?

_____

_____

_____

T Time-bound: When do you want to accomplish this goal?

_____

_____

_____

Expectations ☉ Effect Size of 0.43

Another way to foster growth mindset is to think about expectations. According to Carol Dweck, having high expectations correlates to high student achievement. When we have high expectations for learning, we help students develop the confidence to achieve at high levels. The idea of a self-fulfilling prophecy comes into play here: If you think you can do something, you will, and if you think you cannot do something, you won't. Research has found that when teachers believe their students can achieve, they do indeed achieve. On the other hand, when teachers have low expectations of students, they usually fulfill this expectation as well. This teaches us to be cautious in our interactions with students and to ensure we are promoting a culture of high expectations for achievement.

With the onset of the Common Core Standards, one of the expectations is that schools prepare students to be college- and career-ready. Teachers are expected to teach at higher levels so students can achieve success. Because of this, many schools and districts have begun to talk about setting high expectations and their role in setting learning goals for students and teachers.

High expectations also relate to goal setting and self-efficacy. When you have a culture that promotes high expectations, goal setting and self-efficacy are not far behind. They are the results of having these high expectations.

Building a culture of high expectations requires teachers to have a clear understanding of even the lowest expectations for learning. Once these minimums are established and communicated, teachers can develop goals for learning that are consistent so everyone has the same expectations. One sure way to fall short on accomplishing a culture of high expectations is to have an unclear, inconsistent definition of what high expectations look like.

Success Criteria

Another way to build a culture of high expectations is to set clear expectations for learning by establishing success criteria. These allow students to see what the expectations are so they can judge their progress toward their goals. Success criteria goes hand in hand with rubrics: In order for students to assess where the teacher is trying to take them, it's important to have a clear indication of success and eliminate any guesswork. Teachers can establish success criteria for any and all subject matter. Here's an example:

Learning objective: Write a complete sentence

Step 1: Think of an idea you want to write about.

Step 2: Ensure your sentence has both a subject and verb.

Step 3: Use a capital for the first word of the sentence.

Step 4: Make sure the words are arranged in order.

Step 5: Check to see if the sentence has a complete thought.

Step 6: End the sentence with proper punctuation.

The above example provides students with clear criteria for the expectations of a properly written complete sentence. This is a simple example, but this process can be completed for any subject.

Rubrics

Rubrics are another great tool to use when establishing success criteria. A rubric is a guide that provides students with specific criteria for grading. Rubrics help students anticipate and determine their grade on an assignment before the teacher grades it. They also provide information about the criteria necessary for achieving success. When I was a teacher at the college level, I always gave my students rubrics so they had a road map for success when writing papers.

In recent times, we have started to see more elementary school teachers using rubrics as a way to provide guidance for their students on what success looks like. Here is a sample rubric for a writing assignment that I developed for one of my college classes.

Literary Analysis Rubric
(25 points possible)

You will complete a literary analysis in weeks 2 through 7. Each analysis relates to the culture of focus for the corresponding workshop week. Each analysis will require that you choose 3 texts (children's literature, poetry, etc.) and complete the analysis questions in the course text. Each literary analysis is worth 25 points.

1. Choose three texts that relate to the culture being studied. Texts can include children's literature, poetry, excerpts from novels, etc.

2. Include a synopsis of each text selected.

3. Answer the specified questions in the textbook each week.

4. Submission should be one or two pages in length.

5. Submit the assignment by the due date.

CRITERIA	POINTS POSSIBLE	POINTS EARNED	SPECIFIC FEEDBACK
Student chooses three texts that relate to the specified culture.	5		
Student's response includes a synopsis of the texts and answers the specific questions in the textbook.	15		
Conventions: Student uses APA format, including title page, abstract, introduction, body, conclusion, heading, citations, references, page numbers, etc. Student takes careful attention to grammar.	5		

✎ Reflection

How can success criteria be useful with your kids?

_____

_____

_____

Write an example of success criteria for an upcoming lesson or unit.

_____

_____

_____

How have you used rubrics successfully with your students?

_____

_____

_____

Create a rubric for an upcoming assignment.

_____

_____

_____

Self-Verbalization and Self-Questioning ⟳ Effect Size of 0.64

Another aspect of growth mindset is that students will begin to have greater use of their ability to self-verbalize and self-question, which, according to Hattie, has a positive effect size of 0.64. Self-verbalization and self-questioning refer to the internal dialogue that learners use to clarify their understanding. When students self-verbalize, they express their individual learning out loud. Self-questioning refers to students asking questions of themselves that relate to their learning. Both are intrinsic signs of learning that are specific and individualized to the learner. The highest level of learning is when one can self-direct their learning and ask questions of themselves to improve.

Teachers can help students with their self-questioning and verbalization by modeling the process and by asking clarifying questions to get students to the desired outcome. Here are some examples of questions that lead to self-questioning and self-verbalization.

- What is our objective today?

- How confident are you in your ability to accomplish the goal today?

- How do you rank the activity? (very difficult) (very easy) (just right)

- How did the lesson or activity go?

- Were you correct in your assessment of how you would do on the objective? Why or why not?

- What steps will you take to do better on the objective next time?

The above questions teach students to internally assess their learning before and after a given task. This is an important skill that helps build a growth mindset. As students become more reflective about their own learning, they will be able to take on more challenging tasks.

✎ Reflection

What type of reflection questions do you prepare or plan to prepare for your students?

_____

_____

_____

How can becoming more reflective help your students' achievement?

_____

_____

_____

How can you model this behavior in a future lesson?

_____

_____

_____

Motivation ○ Effect Size of 0.47

With a positive effect size of 0.47, student motivation is an important trait to foster. Students who are motivated to learn have a positive attitude and feel that they are in control of their learning. Motivated students remove obstacles, or see them as merely stepping stones on the pathway to success. Teachers often ask me how they can help their students become motivated learners, but there is no easy answer to this question. Motivation is one of those intrinsic qualities that we often feel people are born with. However, I believe that motivation can be acquired and we can foster it in our students.

Motivational theorists like Fredrick Herzberg conclude that people work harder when they are recognized and enjoy their work. This relates to motivation, because as students are recognized for their efforts, they will become more self-motivated to improve in their practice. We can help our students enjoy their work more by providing opportunities for them to display their work so it can be celebrated. Many classrooms have a wall of excellence where exemplary work samples are displayed. Kids love to see their work displayed. It brings a sense of pride and is a motivating factor to do better.

Another way to motivate students to work harder is to recognize their efforts to grow. This is accomplished by celebrating student success, allowing kids to track their progress toward a goal, and recognizing their efforts as they work toward a final outcome. I have seen this in the form of progress charts, where students color in their progress toward a goal after taking different benchmark assessments. Teachers also use tracking sheets that students keep in a binder and update after each testing period. These binders are then shared with parents during parent teacher conferences. Schools can support this growth mindset by celebrating student growth at whole school assemblies. This has proven to be very effective, as it brings a spotlight to growth at a school-wide level.

One final way to motivate students is to allow them to serve as helpers when they have mastered content. This positive recognition of serving as a helper or teacher's assistant rewards students for their success while letting them grow.

Growth Mindset Recap

Having a growth mindset is a leveling tool in education. If you have a notion that you can do something, you often will accomplish it. On the other hand, if you have a notion you cannot do something, it is likely that you will not. How does the old saying go? If you think you can, you can, and if you think you cannot, you are right.

As educators, our job is to encourage our students to work toward their goals and achieve them. This is accomplished by providing clear success criteria for students, as well as indicators of how they are progressing toward their goals. We also have to work on building a mind frame where the glass is half full instead of half empty. This shift in thinking will allow students to build on their strengths and not focus on their shortcomings.

Additionally, we must learn to embrace failure as a learning tool. Failure is the only way for us to learn and grow better. It is only when we are pushed to our limit that we soar to new levels. Understanding this, instilling it in our students, and taking it on in our own lives will be pivotal in providing sustained success in our schools.

CHAPTER 3

Collaboration and Visible Learning Research

John Hattie has identified teacher collaboration as a high-leverage strategy that can help close the achievement gap, with an exceptional effect size of 1.56. Teacher collaboration helps educators build consensus regrading what success looks like. Collaboration also helps establish agreed-upon areas of focus and levels of rigor on a school campus. It goes beyond one teacher working as a silo; instead, it improves instruction by building a network of expertise. This network is key because the more people who are involved in decisions about learning, the better. Together, teachers come to conclusions about the right things to implement and monitor. Think about medical doctors as they go on rounds. These experts work together to diagnose and come up with treatment plans to improve health. This same concept can come into play in our schools.

According to Hattie's 2015 work, *The Politics of Collaborative Expertise*, collaboration among teachers enables student growth and success. When teachers have a community of collaboration, they are able to share practices that work and discuss data trends, which helps them make more targeted decisions regarding their teaching practices. Again, this collaborative exchange of ideas helps teachers move student learning at much quicker rates than when they work alone.

So, what is the definition of collaboration? Merriam Webster defines collaboration as "[working] jointly with others or together, especially in an intellectual endeavor." When teachers are given time to work collaboratively, and a culture of collaboration is established, they can begin to replicate positive practices and build teacher efficacy. The remainder of this chapter will discuss some key aspects of collaborating, including finding the time to collaborate and building a need for collaboration in your school. There is no right or wrong way to begin the collaboration process, but the key is to have a set time and agreed-upon structure for facilitating true collaboration.

Collaboration can occur at different levels. In this chapter, we will go over some strategies for high-intensity collaboration for teams that are ready to hit the ground running. We will also share some examples of simple ways you can begin working with a team member to first explore the idea of collaborating. Finally, the appendix includes some great articles and books you might want to check out to build on your understanding of collaboration.

How Does Collaboration Benefit Schools?

Schools and systems that foster collaborative cultures can expect to find teachers and staff who have rich conversations about student learning. These conversations are often filled with references to student data and observation. They also tend to focus on solutions and are not typically laced with complaints or excuses. These groups of teachers or teams will have purposeful dialogue about where students are and where they want students to go.

The term professional learning community (PLC) has been all the buzz for decades. PLCs are groups of educators that meet regularly to develop structures that foster collaborative practice.[3] As these groups show us, collaboration does not just happen, but it has to be planned for and expected.

We have known for decades that there is higher achievement in schools where teachers work in teams. However, even though we know this is a best practice, it is not always practiced in our schools. One may wonder why such a high-impact

---

3   Richard DuFour, *Learning by Doing: A Handbook for Professional Learning Communities at Work*, Bloomington, IN: Solution Tree, 2006.

strategy is not occurring. There are many reasons, including lack of time to collaborate, lack of expectations for what collaboration should look like, and teacher apathy.

Teachers often feel overwhelmed and helpless, which can impart apathy. This sense of overwhelm and helplessness can be attributed to many factors, including the high levels of academic rigor we have experienced in recent times. These demands require that teachers provide high levels of instruction for students at differentiated levels. But with collaborative efforts, feelings of apathy can be turned around, and educators can once again feel excited about their work.

Making Time for Collaboration

Time is always of the essence in education. The typical school day is just over six and a half hours, according to the National Center for Education Statistics.[4] This includes lunch, recess, and special classes like physical education, music, or art. If we take out the time for these activities, teachers are left with between four and five and a half hours each day to teach core classes. Some teachers may have prep time built into their day, but unless the school has common prep time, collaboration can be nonexistent. If schools are going to make collaboration a key part of their culture, schedules must be adapted to support this.

In an ideal world, teaches are given common time to collaborate weekly. In my experience, this works best when it occurs during the school day. Teachers often have after-school duty, teach after-school intervention groups, or are simply too exhausted after a long day of teaching to effectively collaborate after school. Including time for collaboration as part of the school schedule marks it as important. If the school does not have time during the day for collaboration, having a set day of the week for teachers to collaborate after school will be sufficient, but again, this time must be kept sacred; other meetings and obligations have to be dismissed so this team collaboration time can be respected. The worst thing a school administrator can do is call meetings during a team's protected collaboration time. Doing so sends a message that team time is not important and that collaboration is not an area of focus for the school.

---

4   National Center for Education Statistics, "Average Length of School Year and Average Length of School Day, by Selected Characteristics: United States, 2003–04," US Department of Education, Accessed December 2017, https://nces.ed.gov/surveys/pss/tables/table_2004_06.asp.

✎ Reflection

Does your school have common planning time for your grade level members?

_____

_____

_____

If you have common planning time, does your grade level team meet on any of these days to collaborate?

_____

_____

_____

If you do not have common planning time, how can you address this with your administrator to encourage them to think about building common planning time into the schedule to support team collaboration?

_____

_____

_____

Are you or your teammates involved in any after-school activities that would hinder you from meeting to collaborate with your team?

_____

_____

_____

How do you see a collaboration meeting running?

_____

_____

_____

What would you see as your role in a collaboration meeting?

_____

_____

_____

What apprehensions, if any, do you have regarding meeting as a collaborative team?

_____

_____

_____

What experience, if any, have you had working with teams?

_____

_____

_____

What did you find most helpful and least helpful about working in teams?

_____

_____

_____

What can collaboration look like?

_____

_____

_____

How might collaborating with higher and lower grade level teams help with instruction?

_____

_____

_____

Suggestions for Collaboration

There is no one-size-fits-all template for what a collaborative team meeting would look like. Collaboration can be a very structured activity, where individuals or teams have specific roles and functions. Ideally, this type of collaboration produces an outcome that teams can use to provide evidence of their team time. A structured model is the most common practice for teams, but it is not the only way that collaboration can work.

Here, I want to explore some ideas for collaboration that are a bit outside the box. The fact is, your school system may not support a structured team collaboration model. You may also have teammates who are not keen on the idea of collaboration. This should not, however, deter your efforts to build a collaborative group on your school campus, since research has indicated it is an important strategy to build student success.

One way you can collaborate is to schedule times to go watch another teacher's class. Have a conversation before you go in to observe, and set clear parameters regarding what your colleague wants you to observe. Then, go to the class with a specific idea of what the teacher wants you to provide feedback on. It can be management, questioning, differentiation, or anything else. While you're observing, focus on the particular area that you and your colleague agreed on, and look for evidence. After the visit, share what you observed and talk about what some next steps may look like to move the teacher and class to the next level. This should be all about moving forward. As you learned in the growth mindset chapter, it is important to always strive to get better.

Reciprocate this activity by having your teammate come in to observe you and provide feedback on whatever strategy or practice they observe. This is a very simple way to build a culture of collaboration. Once your colleagues see you performing this practice, before long, they will begin to want to explore the practice themselves.

To foster advanced collaboration, you and your colleagues might think about switching the times you teach particular subjects to accommodate observation schedules. For example, if your break is during the time your teammate teaches math but she wants you to observe during reading for that day, she could switch her reading time so you could perform the observation. Be sure to inform your administrator if you are going to be switching any subject times so they are aware of the change.

✎ Reflection

List two or three strategies or activities you would like a colleague to provide feedback on.

_____

_____

_____

What, in particular, would you like your teammate to provide feedback on?

_____

_____

_____

Which teammate would you like to approach about trying this collaborative practice with?

_____

_____

_____

What would be a good time to have your colleague come in to observe you?

_____

_____

_____

How will you tell your administrator about your collaborative project? What are some key points you want to provide regarding the importance of this collaborative effort?

_____

_____

_____

What will you do with the feedback you receive from your colleague?

_____

_____

_____

When you go in to observe your colleague, how will you ensure that you are objective and only focus on the requested strategy?

_____

_____

_____

📖 Resource

Sample Peer Observation Form

Write down what is observed:

_____

_____

_____

What went well in the observation?

_____

_____

_____

What are next steps or things to think about?

_____

_____

_____

What questions do you have?

_____

_____

_____

How Do We Get Teachers Excited About Collaboration?

For other teachers to get excited about collaboration, they need access to the research behind the method and why it is such an important practice to employ. As educators, we entered the field of education because we wanted to make a difference in the lives of children. No teacher shows up to school each day wanting their students to fail and be unsuccessful. We all entered into this noble profession to help students succeed.

Today's students come with many different needs. Collaboration provides an opportunity to get feedback from our colleagues about our practices. This helps us make decisions more quickly. We all know that two heads are better than one and it truly takes a village to educate today's students. We live in a fast-paced society where information changes at the speed of light. Our colleagues may have some tools that can benefit our students, and by taking the time to collaborate, we can save ourselves and our students a lot of time in finding solutions. Collaboration provides a village mentality of group support that has been research-proven to really make a difference in moving student achievement.

Until we develop a more open policy of sharing teacher practices, we will continue to see some classrooms soaring while others are left struggling. As a teacher, I was always collaborative and looked for ways to improve my practice. I wanted to be in my colleagues' classrooms and I wanted them in mine so we could navigate the curriculum together. I knew there was strength in numbers. I had learned this from my years playing team sports. I'm a product of the '80s and love Michael Jordan, but I always remember he did not win championships until he built his team. Education teams must also come together so they can level the playing field for their kids.

It may take time to build a case for collaboration with some of your colleagues. Discussing the research about the positive effects of collaboration is a great place to start. I have included some articles and websites at the end of the book that you can use to start this conversation.

Case Study

Elizabeth was a pull-out English language learners (ELL) teacher in an urban elementary school in Nashville, TN. One of her kindergarten students, Alex, lacked basic phonemic awareness and phonics skills. As a result, he was below grade level in reading. To help Alex, Elizabeth partnered with Mrs. Blackmoore, Alex's self-contained classroom teacher, to create an individualized learning plan. The plan started with assessment. Elizabeth assessed Alex's language skills and Mrs. Blackmoore assessed Alex's literacy skills. The teachers shared the results with one another and used the information to tailor Alex's small group and one-on-one instruction. In addition, Elizabeth and Mrs. Blackmoore touched base with each other once a week to discuss Alex's progress. They also used this time to share ideas about how they could improve their instruction.

By the end of the year, the teachers' collaborative efforts paid off. Not only did Alex acquire phonemic awareness and phonics skills, he was reading on grade level and set to test out of ELL services the next year. Elizabeth was overjoyed with Alex's success. She knew that without collaboration, it would not have been possible. From that point forward, Elizabeth made collaboration a professional priority.

Collaboration can be a most powerful leveling tool for students and can help make huge differences for students in need. The practice of collaboration can help accelerate growth and problem solving in cases where time is of the essence.

CHAPTER 4

Teacher Clarity and Visible Learning Research

Teacher clarity is the ability for teachers to be clear on what they are teaching and what they want students to accomplish. It is also important for students, who need to have clarity on the expectations for their learning in order to perform at high levels of achievement. Clearly displayed expectations take away any confusion about an assignment, for both students and teachers. By providing clear expectations for success, teachers can easily assess the progress the class is making toward achieving the desired outcome, and students can assess their individual progress.

In this chapter, you will explore teacher clarity and the tools you can use to implement this strategy in your teaching. Learning targets, success criteria, explicit instruction, and checking for understanding each provide opportunities for students to obtain clearly defined expectations for learning.

Why Is Teacher Clarity So Important?

Teacher clarity has an impressive positive effect size of 0.75. John Hattie and Dylan Wiliam, an educational researcher focused on helping educators use assessments effectively, both conclude that having clear expectations for learning accelerates student growth. Hattie states that teacher clarity is an important instructional tool that educators should embrace because it provides direction in learning.

Wiliam notes that in order for students to succeed in their learning, they must know what steps are expected to be taken for any given assignment or task.[5] This goes beyond just posting an objective on the board and repeating it in unison; for years, we have had compliance mandates to post learning objectives in our classroom. Simply having an objective posted does not guarantee that students are cognizant of the learning expectations. I am as guilty as anyone in posting learning objectives for the sake of learning objectives, but we need to step back and think about these learning objectives.

Learning objectives are important because they provide a road map for the teacher and student to understand where the lesson is going. In my career, I have observed lessons that are not at all related to the learning objective the teacher has identified. In reflective conversations I've had with the teachers, they often think that they have addressed the objective but later realize that they did not. By making a conscious effort to have clarity, teachers can improve on providing clearly focused lessons that address the desired outcomes.

Clarity in the Classroom

Teacher clarity involves having a structured, set way of introducing the lessons so that there is no confusion about what is expected for the learners. This involves setting clear learning objectives with success criteria that aligns to the course objectives. Teachers that have clarity are masters at providing students with expectations and criteria that are measurable and achievable. In classrooms

---

5   Dylan Wiliam, *Leadership for Teacher Learning: Creating a Culture Where All Teachers Improve So That All Students Succeed*, West Palm Beach, FL: Learning Sciences International, 2016.

where there is teacher clarity, students are easily able to explain what they are learning, and they have clear knowledge of how they are being graded. There are no surprises. Teachers assess based on content as it is covered in the current lesson.

Teachers with clarity explicitly state, and often repeat, their instructions for assignments to ensure students understand. This looks like a teacher checking for understanding as they are teaching. They continually ask questions to ensure students understand the directions and are clear on the expectations. When a teacher does this masterfully, it is not seen as a mundane process, but is a natural way to communicate expectations. In my experience as a college English professor, this was especially important when assigning essays. Students often had misconceptions about what I expected in the writing assignment. I would take the time to explicitly state the expectations and would also take time to answer any clarifying questions from my students. If you are working with elementary students, this skill may have to be taught, as students often do not know what question to ask for clarification. You can help them out by asking them to explain the directions or expectations to a neighbor as you go around and listen to ensure there are no misconceptions.

Teacher Clarity and Guided Practice

Guided practice is a great way to ensure clarity in the classroom. This can look like you providing sample problems or questions for students to answer, and guiding them through the process of responding. During these guided practices, it is important to remember that you want to have dialogue so that any misconceptions can be cleared up immediately. Another key to keep in mind is that guided practice should be exactly that: guided. You do not want to release students to work independently until you are sure they are clear on the process and can confidently perform the task independently. This requires that you check for understanding, which we'll talk about in a later section, to ensure students are with you and ready to move forward.

One last note about guided practice is that it requires you to choose questions that are high-leverage and will provide a basis for more advanced work. You don't want the guided practice to be at a lower level than the independent practice, because students will not be able to transfer the knowledge to the subsequent task. Ensure that the guided and independent practice are aligned so you can have a smooth transition of skills and knowledge.

Here are some statements you can use to check how much clarity you have as a teacher.

I ensure that I teach my lessons in chunks and check for understanding 80 percent of the time.	Yes	No
I use quick checks as often as possible in my teaching.	Yes	No
I know how well my students are performing on a task 80 percent of the time.	Yes	No
I am aware of the deficits in learning my students have.	Yes	No
I ensure all students understand the directions before I move on.	Yes	No
I use rubrics and others tools so students can assess their own learning.	Yes	No

Set Learning Objectives

Clear learning objectives define what students are expected to learn and describe how they will exhibit the desired outcome. There has been much debate regarding how to write learning objectives. Some believe that learning objectives should include the percentage of students that will master the concept. Some believe learning objectives should include the task and activity that will be completed. Others believe learning objectives should merely include the standard that should be met.

I have seen objectives written on the board or on the student worksheet. I have seen teachers who have kids write objectives in their notebooks, and I have also seen teachers who have students read objectives aloud. All of these are ways to bring attention to the learning objective, but do they constitute clarity? Think about traditions you may have practiced in life. I remember reciting the pledge of allegiance every day growing up as a child. I knew the pledge and could say it with cadence, but I never thought about what the words meant. I merely memorized it and repeated it each morning before school.

I challenge you to think about ways to clarify your learning objectives so that you and your students are clear on what the learning expectations are. Ways to do this include using rubrics or models to show students examples of what you expect, or having students paraphrase the objective so you can ensure their understanding. Use these statements to check the effectiveness of your learning objectives.

My students repeat the learning objective.	Yes	No
I go over the learning objective at the beginning of each lesson.	Yes	No
My learning objectives are based on the activities or standards we are going to address during the lesson.	Yes	No
My students can articulate the learning objective in their own words 80 percent of the time.	Yes	No
I ensure that I have a learning objective posted for each lesson that I teach 90 percent of the time.	Yes	No
I carefully craft learning objectives and revise them as needed.	Yes	No
Learning objectives help drive the activities and lessons that I teach.	Yes	No

Success Criteria

Success criteria is all the buzz in education today. Success criteria provides specific and measurable definitions of what is expected in learning.

SUCCESS CRITERIA	LEARNING OBJECTIVE
I can explain how global warming affects the environment by providing three examples from the text.	Students will understand global warming and its impact on the environment.

In the above example, the success criteria is clear because it clearly defines what success looks like. Success will be measured when students are able to go into the text to find examples to support their responses regarding global warming.

However, the learning objective is unclear. It simply states that students will understand global warming, but this objective is not measurable or concrete.

Both learning objectives and success criteria are important in learning. Many teachers include both in the lessons that they teach. The objective provides the focus for the lesson, and the success criteria serves as a driving force behind the assessment of the objective.

✎ Reflection

Look back in your lesson plans and determine if the learning objectives you provided had success criteria. What did you find?

_____

_____

_____

Rewrite three objectives to include success criteria.

_____

_____

_____

How will success criteria help clarify understanding for your students?

_____

_____

_____

How will writing clear learning objectives and success criteria help make your lesson more effective?

_____

_____

_____

Explicit Instruction and Teacher Clarity

One strategy to ensure clarity is to use explicit instructional practices, including guiding students through the learning process by scaffolding and modeling activities. In this guided approach, clarity is obtained because teachers do not move students to independent practice until students are clear on the expectations and can perform them independently.

Explicit instruction requires that teachers slow down the teaching process to ensure all students acquire the learning. This ensures that they only move forward when students are ready. Explicit instructional practices can be used in teaching any subject. The key is to know the learner and respond to their needs. This approach also requires time to reflect and review so that lessons can be monitored and adjusted as needed.

EXPLICIT INSTRUCTION	LECTURE
Direct approach to teaching	Indirect approach
Embedded practice	No practice
Clearly state learning objectives and expectations	General explanation of what is expected
Modeled practice	Limited practice

✎ Reflection

Is your teaching style more direct and explicit, or do you tend to lecture?

_____

_____

_____

What are some subjects where you can employ more direct instruction?

_____

_____

_____

How can you make explicit instruction engaging?

_____

_____

_____

What reservations, if any, do you have about using direct instruction techniques?

_____

_____

_____

Checking for Understanding

One way to determine if your students are indeed understanding a concept or lesson is to check what they've learned. Checking for understanding allows the teacher to monitor and adjust their instruction as needed. It helps them determine when students are struggling or already have the knowledge necessary to move on to the next topic. Checking for understanding allows the teacher to quickly clear up any misconceptions and determine if a student merely made a mistake or has a more substantial misunderstanding about the topic.

When you check for understanding, you have to pose questions that can allow you to assess your students' abilities. The questions posed should lend themselves to immediate interpretation of student understanding. Merely asking "Who needs more time?" or "Did you understand the question?" will not get you where you want to go. Instead, ask questions and have kids share their responses. Some ways to do this include providing white boards or having students use online tools, like Plickers. These allows the teacher to quickly check to see who got the answer correct and who did not. I see this done a lot in math classes, but it can also work in reading and other content areas.

The key to checking understanding is posing questions that target the most pivotal content standard or skill within a unit before moving on to another topic. Most teachers ask these questions as multiple choice questions or true/false questions. They do this so that they can quickly scan the room to see who got the question right or wrong. It's helpful to occasionally mix up the format of the questions; for example, you can sometimes ask open response questions that require more elaboration. This way, you can see the thought process and assess student understanding at a more in-depth level.

Here are some suggested formats for quick checking for understanding tasks and tools.

1. True or false questions

2. Plickers

3. Quick response (QR) codes

4. Use white boards and have students hold up their responses

5. Quick write

6. Quick sweep around the room to check on student work

7. Question stems (The correct answer is _____,

   because _____.)

8. Share the wrong answer and have students tell you why it is incorrect.

9. Entry slip

10. Exit slip

11. Fist to five (students show on their hand how they feel about the content, fist meaning "I do not get it," five fingers meaning "I understand completely.")

12. Rubric

13. Face chart to represent understanding: happy face, neutral face, sad face

14. Green, red, and yellow lights to represent understanding

15. 3-2-1 (3 things I understand, 2 things I have a question about, and 1 thing I do not understand)

Teacher Clarity Recap

Teacher clarity is a high-yield strategy that can be used to increase student achievement. The key is to provide the tools so that kids can be self-sufficient learners and responsible for their own teaching. When teachers are clear about expectations and provide opportunities for students to self-assess, reflect, and share their understanding, student achievement soars.

Teacher clarity empowers students to be self-directed and self-corrective in their learning endeavors. Our goal as educators is to empower our students by providing them the tools to work independently and continue on their journey of learning long after they exit our classrooms. The term "lifelong learner" ties in with clarity, because lifelong learners have clear understandings of their educational strengths and are competent in finding ways to improve in their learning and practices when necessary.

CHAPTER 5

Parent Communication and Visible Learning Research

Parents are essential partners in our efforts to educate students and provide support for future generations. As an educator with over 20 years of experience, I can attest to the pivotal role parents play in helping students receive a quality education. Parents are a child's first teachers, and if we can empower them to understand their role, we can see substantial positive change. We cannot control what goes on outside of our classroom doors, but we can provide parents with tools to help ensure students maintain a positive connection between home and school, which can be effective in raising student achievement.

In this chapter, we will focus on some strategies, tips, and programs to employ and share with parents that have been proven to help move student achievement forward. The strategies include preschool programs, parental involvement, and play programs. Additionally, we'll discuss home environment and socioeconomic status. Along with each strategy, you'll learn how parents can use these strategies to assist in student learning.

Preschool Programs ☼ Effect Size of 0.45

Enrollment in a preschool program is one of the greatest gifts a parent can provide for their child's future education. I am a strong proponent for early education because I have seen firsthand the advantage it provides. We know that the earlier we provide support and enrichment for children, the better. This is especially true for students coming from lower socioeconomic areas. There is a substantial vocabulary gap between the rich and the poor. According to Dr. Anne Fernald, this vocabulary gap begins in infancy. Studies show that students who attend preschool enter kindergarten with better pre-reading skills and richer vocabularies, which helps to propel their success.[6] Having children in preschool programs is a great way to begin to level the playing field.

Preschool helps children get a head start on learning. Teachers are able to identify student needs at an earlier time, which in turn allows intervention to occur more quickly. This saves time and effort later on. If a teacher or parent can identify a student area of deficit in preschool, they get an earlier start in providing necessary resources and assistance. Early education programs also help students learn to socialize, which will reduce anxiety when they start kindergarten.

When recommending preschool programs to parents, seek out those that provide social and academic activities. Parents want a well-rounded program that will educate the whole child. An ideal program will have a rich environment that supports student growth, as well as a standardized, connected curriculum. Programs that include music, dance, and other artistic activities are also promising, because these activities help with brain development in students. Music can be used to memorize important information, and dance provides oxygen to the brain, which helps with processing information. Besides these benefits, creative activities provide a fun way to learn, which is important for children.

Not all preschool programs are created equal. Suggest that parents take the time to research the programs and talk to other parents who have children in the program. You can gain a lot of information about the effectiveness of a program by talking to families who are already enrolled. Offer the preschool program evaluation guide, below, as assistance.

---

6   Anne Fernald, et al, "SES Differences in Language Processing Skill and Vocabulary Are Evident at 18 Months," *Developmental Science* 16, no. 2 (2012): 234-248, doi: 10.1111/desc.12019.

📖 Resource

Give these questions to parents to help them evaluate different preschool programs.

1. What is the philosophy of the preschool program? Does the program support academics and provide students with opportunities to be prepared for school?

2. Does the school provide opportunities for fine motor development? Fine motor development is essential for preparing students to write, feed themselves, and take care of basic needs, like buttoning clothing.

3. How does the school promote literacy development? Check to see if the children are immersed in print and if there are opportunities for students to have story time and access to books.

4. Are there opportunities for play time and building skills on working with others? It is important that students are offered the opportunity to play and build their social skills. Preschool-age children need these important skills to be successful when they enter kindergarten.

5. Is there a 1:10 teacher to student ratio? The National Association of Early Childhood Education suggests having a 1:10 student-to-teacher ratio in preschool. When classes are larger than this, students do not get the necessary attention they need to be successful.

6. Is the environment friendly and child focused? Observe children and teachers and see how the environment feels. Are children joyful and learning? Is staff responsive to student needs? Having a safe and warm learning environment is pivotal.

7. Does the school offer opportunities for students to go on field trips? Quality preschool programs provide opportunities for kids to go to museums or community locations, like the grocery store or bakery, so that children can connect to their world. These field trips provide opportunities to build vocabulary and connect what has been read in stories to the real world.

8. Does the school provide an open-door policy for parent input and participation in the program? In order for parents to be a partner in their child's education, they need a supportive school that believes in collaboration

between parents and the school. Check to see how involved parents are in the program and how the school works to bring parents in.

Parental Involvement ☼ Effect Size of 0.51

Parental involvement touts an impressive effect size of 0.51. With such a high correlation to academic success, it is important to encourage parental involvement. This can come in the form of volunteering, engaging in academic programs at the school, and showing a keen interest in the child's learning. Schools can share information with parents regarding the importance of parent involvement and student growth and can make concerted efforts to make parents feel welcome to come into the school. Having parent curriculum nights, sending home parent communication newsletters (print or digital), and inviting parents in during the school day are all ways to support parental involvement and build a sense of community.

Of course, some parents do not feel comfortable coming to school, so we have to find ways to promote involvement for those that will not or cannot show up. Schools must look into parent communication tools that bring parents into the conversation about what is going on in the school. Discussing how parents help at home is a great start.

There is no one-size-fits-all solution for parental involvement. The degree to which parents are involved can vary, but one thing is certain—it leads to amazing gains in student learning. I have worked in some districts with high socioeconomic levels and some with lower socioeconomic levels, where parent involvement has been exhibited in different ways, but one thing is constant: When parents are involved, they take an interest in their child's grades and want to know how they can help at home. These parents ask for extra work over the breaks and want to know about tutoring opportunities if their child is struggling with a concept. Engaging all parents in this way is the goal so we can have more constant success in our schools.

Parent partnership programs have great success when they are executed well. One parent partner program I observed allowed parents to take classes at night, along with their children, where they learned strategies to use at home with their children. The program focused on reading and math strategies for grades

K through 8, and it was very successful because parents were allowed to bring their children with them and practice the strategies with a trained professional. The beauty of the partnership was that parents were surveyed to determine what skills and strategies they felt they needed help with. Providing parents with this power helped validate their importance and their role as their child's first teacher.

Play Programs ○ Effect Size of 0.50

One way that parents can assist their children is to enroll them in play programs. Play programs have a 0.50 positive effect size on achievement. These programs allow students to interact with others and learn to problem solve. Many play programs also provide opportunities for students to develop their academic skills; these programs are based on academics, like a chess club or robotics program. Play programs can also help boost student health. Kids need exercise to produce endorphins and to help build their bones and muscles. I was a student athlete and I found that this helped me develop an outlet for reducing my stress; it also helped focus me when I needed to wind down after a long day of studying.

Additionally, children need play programs to develop their social skills, which will help them in the future when they enter the workforce. Play programs work on important team-building skills that teach students to come to consensus and work through challenges.

Having a balanced education involves having outlets beyond schoolwork. Parents can provide a huge boost for their student's achievement by providing play programs for their youth. Unfortunately, most schools have had to cut their play programs due to time constraints. Many schools do not have art and music programs. However, there are many opportunities for free play programs through local city parks and recreation departments. Parents can often find help at their local recreation center for information about age-appropriate play programs. If they are looking for educational programs, local colleges and universities often provide school-age programs during the summer and sometimes on the weekends. They can also check with their local museums, which also provide summer activities in the arts for children.

📖 Resource

Use these questions with parents to evaluate the appropriateness of a play program for a child.

1. Is the program academically based? Check to see what type of academic focus the program supports. Pick programs that have a theoretical base that will support learning.

2. If the program is non-academic, discover the core beliefs and foundation of the program. Programs may support teamwork, sharing, community involvement, or volunteerism, to name a few. Check to see what core values the program supports.

3. What are the qualifications of the instructors or facilitators? Check to see what type of training the facilitators, coaches, or teachers receive. This is important because you want to ensure that the program is being monitored by quality, trained individuals who will provide the best experience possible for your children.

4. Does the program have any external funding sources? This question may seem odd, but it will provide information for you on some of the hidden philosophies or tenets that may affect the program outcomes. For example, if a program is funded by a recycling company, the program may have a focus on building awareness of the importance of keeping our world green.

5. How long has the organization or program been in existence? This question will provide important information regarding the longevity of a program. Programs evolve over time, and it takes about three years for a program to come to its full potential. This should not be used to rule out a program, but will provide information for you regarding where a program is in its developmental process so you can possibly help grow the program.

Home Environment ⏱ Effect Size of 0.57

Having a positive home environment plays a huge role in student achievement, especially when that environment promotes learning. I was recently in a training on ways to bring books into the home. Research shows that homes with books have students who are more likely to be high achieving. Though this is one of those factors we do not have any control over, we can provide parents with information about the importance of building a supportive home environment that encourages reading and writing, discussing issues, and promotes a growth mindset. Parents are our educational partners, and by providing information on ways they can make their homes education friendly, we can yield high results.

There has been a lot of talk about home environment and student progress in school. Unfortunately, most of this research has been about adverse home experiences and student failure. The beauty of Hattie's research is that it highlights how a positive home environment can quickly help students improve in their achievement. Parents want what is best for their children, but they often do not know what to do to make a huge impact. Providing information on ways to promote learning in their home is great first step.

Here are some suggestions you can provide to parents to help them promote a learning environment in their homes.

1. Have books available in the home, both fiction and non-fiction, so your child can have access to rich literature.

2. Work on math problems in the real world, like when you are cooking or shopping in the grocery store.

3. Use challenging vocabulary words with your children. Rather than baby words, use robust language to promote vocabulary development.

4. Take your children to museums and other cultural venues to build their background knowledge.

5. Invest in a good dictionary and a set of encyclopedias. This may seem old-school, but kids needs to access these materials to develop a love for learning. Reference books allow them to explore topics of interest.

6. Use education apps to promote learning.

7. Watch programs together and discuss what you learn.

8. When you go to the mall, an amusement park, or any other venue that has a map, allow your children to explore the map and talk about directions and map keys.

Socioeconomic Status ○ Effect Size of 0.57

We have long known that students from higher socioeconomic status have greater success in learning, partly because parents in higher socioeconomic areas often have received more education than those of lower socioeconomic status. This is a factor teachers cannot control. However, we can provide the tips noted in the earlier sections, like how to enroll students in preschool and play programs, and how to create an environment for learning in the home. We can also teach parents to employ strategies to promote learning. These strategies can be used by all parents, regardless of socioeconomic status. Here is a list of low- to no-cost practices you can share with parents to help bridge the gap.

1. Get a library card and take your kids to the library weekly.

2. Go to the museum with your children at least once per month. Many museums offer culture passes through the local library; these provide free admission to local museums.

3. Arrange to have a tour of a local bakery or grocery store. Many places of business are happy to offer tours. Use this as an opportunity to share a new experience with your children.

4. If your child is struggling with a concept, hire a tutor. Many high school students and college students are looking for extra money and they can be a great source for tutoring at a very low cost.

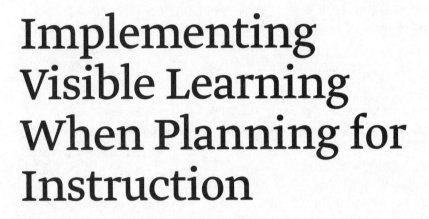
Implementing Visible Learning When Planning for Instruction

As an educator, one of the most important parts of your job is planning for instruction. Your instructional plan will guide your teaching and provide the basis for the activities, responses, and clarity in any given lesson. That being said, high-level instructional planning goes beyond just planning activities. It involves pedagogical understanding of the content being presented, and requires that teachers present this learning in a systematic, structured, and logical manner.

This brings to mind the discussion of the art and science of teaching. We know that quality planning incorporates artful teaching methods; as educators, we consider the nuances in the way we reach our kids, and we ensure that our lessons are engaging and have flair. However, the true nuts and bolts of planning are scientific in nature. This involves ensuring that the strategies we are using are research validated and that we are careful to structure lessons in ways to promote student learning.

When I was a teacher, I remember spending hours upon hours planning for instruction. I wanted to make sure that I planned lessons that were not only engaging, but that were rigorous and would meet the needs of all the different learners in my classroom. I was cognizant of my students' abilities, so I had to think about differentiation. I also had to consider what I wanted them to learn and how I was going to have them demonstrate that learning.

Differentiation is not something that comes naturally for some teachers. Let's face it, it takes a lot of time and planning to effectively differentiate to meet the needs of all learners. As such, differentiation is the number one complaint and stressor for many teachers. It is expected, and we know it is effective, but the time and effort required can sometimes deter teachers from implementing differentiation plans. With careful structures to enhance your planning, you will find that differentiation becomes easier and enjoyable to plan for.

As you plan for instruction, there are many things to keep in mind: determining the focus of the lesson or activity that you are going to present, putting thought into the type of questions you are going to ask, and thinking about how you will assess whether students indeed learned the content that was presented. This chapter will focus on how to incorporate those ideas into your planning while also helping you aim for differentiated instruction. In this chapter, we will discuss strategies for planning and instruction, including classroom discussion, reciprocal teaching, spaced vs. mass practice, metacognitive strategies, direct instruction, and student-centered teaching. Each of these strategies yield at least a year's worth of growth for students.

Classroom Discussion ○ Effect Size of 0.82

Classroom discussion refers to the opportunity for students to converse with their classmates about educational topics. This activity helps students clarify their understanding and also provides an opportunity for them to hear another student's thinking on a topic, which has been proven to help kids test their ideas and opinions against those of others. These are pivotal skills students need to master in order to build their understanding of complex ideas. Classroom discussions have also been proven to help students retain learning.

▦ Procedure

1. Look over your lesson and decide on points in the lesson when you will have students discuss key ideas. Decide on a topic that you want your students to discuss.

2. Think of three to four talking points you want your students to cover during their discussion. These talking points should align with the most important curricular focus of the standard being taught. For example, you might ask students to discuss the importance of women gaining the right to vote. In this example, women's rights is the primary curricular focus of the discussion.

3. Write down the questions that you will ask your students to discuss. This pre-planning will ensure that you are asking the right questions to get to the level of understanding or focus of debate you have planned for.

4. Share your ground rules for debate. These ground rules may include listening to a classmate's point of view and repeating their thought before building on to the discussion.

> ✐ **HELPFUL HINT** You cannot have an appropriate classroom discussion without proper planning. In order for your students to get the most of your classroom discussion, ensure that your pre-planned questions are aligned with where you want to lead students. Don't ask questions that will take the kids down a rabbit hole. Rather, focus your questions on the key concepts, ideas, and standards that you want to target.

5. Conduct your classroom debate. Always end the discussion by sharing the key thoughts and ideas that surfaced from the discussion.

✎ Reflection

What are your thoughts on using classroom discussions?

_____

_____

_____

_____

What experience, if any, have you had with classroom discussions?

_____

_____

_____

_____

Classroom discussion had an effect size of 0.82, which means that it has the potential to really accelerate learning in your classroom. How will you work to build time for classroom discussions?

_____

_____

_____

_____

What challenges do you see in implementing classroom discussions with your students?

_____

_____

_____

_____

What benefits do you see in implementing classroom discussions?

_____

_____

_____

_____

What steps will you take to start using classroom discussions with your students?

_____

_____

_____

_____

What subject will most easily lend itself to using classroom discussions?

_____

_____

_____

_____

📖 Resource

Use these prompts to help plan a discussion for the classroom.

Unit Title: _____

Date(s): _____

Objectives: _____

Discussion question #1

_____

_____

_____

Discussion question #2:

_____

_____

_____

Discussion question #3:

_____

_____

_____

Discussion question #4:

_____

_____

_____

Discussion Summary:

_____

_____

_____

Reciprocal Teaching ○ Effect Size of 0.74

Reciprocal teaching involves segmenting text into sections so that meaningful dialogue can occur between the teacher and students. This requires a lot of planning, because teachers must pre-read the text and find distinct concepts in the book so they can stop to initiate conversations. In this model, the students become the teachers as they lead the discussions. Again, it takes a lot of planning to ensure that the students are ready to take on this important role. With an effect size of 0.74, it is certainly a strategy to plan for and execute in the classroom.

⊞ Procedure

1. Pre-read the text that you are going to have students work on for their dialogue.

2. Mark up any places in the text where you can ask students to work on the skills of clarifying, visualizing, questioning, summarizing, and predicting.

3. Model for students what clarifying means. For example, pick a vocabulary word and show the students how you clarify the meaning of the word.

4. Model how to visualize what is happening in the text and how this helps you comprehend meaning. For example, if a character is providing details about where they live, demonstrate how you use your imagination to visualize the setting and how this helps bring you into the story more, which aids in comprehension.

5. Model questioning by choosing a section of the book where a good question can be asked. For example, why did the character behave in this manner?

6. Model summarizing for students by summarizing a section of the reading.

7. Model predicting by choosing a specific point in the text where there is ambiguity, and show how you can predict an outcome. This modeling may take place over the span of a few lessons if your students are not catching on to it very quickly. You may find that the summarizing and clarifying steps may move more quickly, as these are skills that students tend to master at higher rates.

8. Once you are satisfied that your students have mastered these steps, you can move them toward clarifying, visualizing, questioning, summarizing, and predicting on their own in a group. Planning comes into play here again, as you will have to find texts that lend themselves to all of the strategies listed above. You can use this as a planned activity when students are learning new information in any subject matter.

HELPFUL HINT Planning for reciprocal teaching requires that you read and re-read texts and think about your students and their thought processes. I suggest getting together about five texts that you can use and having them readily available. You may have to scrap some of them if students are not grasping the concepts. This can happen if the text is about something kids don't have any background knowledge on, or if the text is at too complicated a reading level for independent reading. The best thing to do is to practice this teaching method a few times so you can eventually set kids off to do it independently.

✎ Reflection

Write about a time you used reciprocal teaching in your classroom.

_____

_____

_____

What are the benefits of reciprocal teaching?

_____

_____

_____

What are some challenges you anticipate in planning for reciprocal teaching? How will you combat those challenges?

_____

_____

_____

After your first reciprocal teaching lesson, write about what went well and what you will do to make the lesson better next time.

_____

_____

_____

📖 Resource

Use these prompts to plan a reciprocal teaching session.

Name of text:_____

Point in text where you can ask a clarifying question about vocabulary:

_____

_____

Point in text where you can ask students to visualize:

_____

_____

Point in text where you can ask a question:

_____

_____

Point in text where you will stop to have students summarize:

_____

_____

Point in text where you will stop to have students predict an outcome:

_____

_____

Metacognitive Strategies
○ Effect Size of 0.69

Metacognition has often been referred to as thinking about thinking; when using metacognitive strategies, we think about what we are thinking when completing a task. Metacognition can be used when teaching any subject, and it can be used for several purposes. For example, metacognition can be used to determine how to complete a task, to monitor progress on completing a task, and to evaluate progress on learning a task.

Metacognitive strategies provide teachers with the opportunity to share their thinking so that it comes alive for students. Teachers that model all of these thinking processes provide necessary learning strategies that students will use to build success throughout their learning career.

▦ Procedure

1. Before teaching a metacognitive strategy, let students know that you are going to model your thinking process as you complete a task.

2. It can be helpful to write down the steps of your thought process so students can break down the learning in real time.

3. Complete a small piece of the task and tell students what your internal thought process was while completing the task.

4. Complete a second part of the task and again verbalize what your thought process was while completing task.

5. Continue this process until the task is complete.

6. Ask students to share any questions they have about the thought process that you modeled.

7. You may be surprised at the questions that you get. Students often clarify their misunderstandings as they ask you to elaborate on your thought process.

HELPFUL HINT Before conducting any lesson on metacognitive learning, make sure that you practice the task several times and write down explicitly what you are thinking during each step. Humans are skilled learners, so comprehending a text or performing a math operation comes naturally to us. It takes effort to be mindful of our thinking and to slow down to ensure our metacognitive model is complete. I often share my metacognitive lessons with my colleagues before I present it to my class so they can help me fill in any missing gaps.

✎ Reflection

Do you feel anxious about modeling your thinking? If so, why?

_____

_____

_____

What would be a benefit of bringing your thinking to the forefront in your lesson?

_____

_____

_____

What are two to three lessons where using metacognitive strategies would be useful?

_____

_____

_____

Commit to presenting at least one metacognitive lesson in the next week. After you compete the lesson, reflect on your experience.

_____

_____

_____

📖 Resource

Here are some sample prompts for a lesson involving metacognitive practices.

I am thinking... _____

_____

I am wondering..._____

_____

I am feeling... _____

_____

I predict... _____

_____

I am noticing..._____

_____

My first step is to... _____

_____

My next step is to... _____

_____

I check my work by... _____

_____

If I make a mistake, I... _____

_____

I move on when... _____

_____

Direct Instruction ☼ Effect Size of 0.59

Direct instruction is a skills-oriented teaching method that, as its name implies, is directly taught by the teacher. During direct instruction, teachers break the content into small, manageable pieces that are sequenced and explicitly taught. This type of teaching is not a passive activity. Teachers provide guided instruction that is targeted in order to avoid any misinterpretation by students.

Direct instruction is one of the oldest teaching methods, in which a teacher uses a script to teach a lesson or skill. In modern times, direct instruction has been associated with scripted reading and writing programs. Although direct instruction has been criticized as being rigid, research has shown it is a very successful teaching method for instructing learners.

⊞ Procedure

1. After assessing your students, determine an area of focus for your lesson.

2. Make sure that your focus is narrow and not too big. Concentrate the material that you will be teaching on only one major strategy or skill.

3. Introduce the strategy or skill by explicitly telling students what they are going to be learning during the lesson.

4. Let the students know what your expectations are and how they will know they have achieved them.

5. Provide clear examples and non-examples as you are teaching the lesson. These examples need to be concrete and must correlate directly with your intended focus.

6. Model the correct way to perform the task or skill. As you are modeling, show each step in a deliberate manner.

7. Have the students repeat the steps along with you. Do not move on until all students can repeat the steps of the task.

✎ Reflection

What are your reservations about using direct instruction in your teaching?

_____

_____

_____

HELPFUL HINT   Direct instruction has gotten a bad name in recent years. Many have called it passé and old-school, but according to Hattie's research, it is an effective method of teaching students. I do not advocate for using direct instruction in every lesson, but when there are tasks that need to be mastered and that lend themselves to this model of teaching, you have a strong research base behind you to prove that it will be a successful way to reach your learners.

Teachers often feel self-conscious when they are modeling deliberately. Keep in mind that your students are often seeing content for the first time and they need the repetition that the direct instructional model provides. Try to think back to a time when you were learning a new skill. If you keep this in mind, you will be able to see how important modeling and direct instruction is for helping your students master learning.

What is a lesson that you can teach this week where the direct instruction model will be appropriate? Break down the task or skill that you are going to teach into manageable chunks.

_____

_____

_____

📖 Resource

Fill out these prompts as a starting point for a lesson using direct instruction.

Subject: _____

Standard: _____

Skill assessed: _____

Objective:

The students will...

_____

_____

Pre-Assessment

Room setup:

_____

_____

Materials needed:

_____

_____

Direct instruction content:

_____

_____

Strategies to be taught:

_____

_____

Introduction/hook:

_____

_____

Guided practice:

_____

_____

Scaffolding independent practice:

_____

_____

Assessment

Teacher reflection about next steps:

_____

_____

_____

_____

Spaced Practice ○ Effect Size of 0.71

When you provide spaced, or spiraled, practice, you offer students the opportunity to practice what they have learned over the course of their schooling (in previous years and semesters), not just what they are learning in that particular week or quarter. Mass practice refers to students reviewing only what they have learned more recently.

Spaced practice allows students to practice learning from the current and past few chapters so those ideas remain fresh and established. Research finds that when teachers provide these types of experiences, students retain the information better. Think about the formative assessments that we take to get into college. The SAT and ACT both have questions that test students on their overall learning experience from primary, middle, and high school. Other standardized assessments also follow this model.

▦ Procedure

1. If you work in a school system, look at your curriculum map or standards pacing calendar. If you do not work for a school, look at the standards and determine a logical pace for the unit you are planning for.

2. Use the mapping tool on page 68 (or create a map of your own) to map out the standards to align with your curriculum plan.

3. Once your alignment is complete, look at your map and fill in ideas for spacing out elements of the curriculum or providing opportunities to revisit standards that build on others.

4. Use the mapping tool to determine times to practice important standards that you want your class to reinforce.

5. Once your mapping document is complete, review it to make sure that you have a logical spiraled practice embedded in your instructional plan.

HELPFUL HINT Spiraling your instructional practice requires intentional planning time. You have to keep abreast of the standards and skills and how they build on one another. A good thing to keep in mind is that you can talk to teachers from the grade levels below you to get ideas of which standards the kids really need to master to be successful. I would also suggest talking to the teacher in the grade level above you to see what initial skills they think students should enter their classroom with. Having these cross-curricular conversations and fostering teacher collaboration are key to building a strong foundation that continues for your students throughout their learning career.

✎ Reflection

What are the most important standards or skills you need to teach in your next unit of study?

_____

_____

_____

What are the supporting standards that kids will need to practice in this unit?

_____

_____

_____

How can you map out a plan to include both the essential and supporting standards?

_____

_____

_____

Write or find five practice questions that relate to your current standard.

_____

_____

_____

Write or find four practice questions that relate to important previous standards.

_____

_____

_____

📖 Resource

Fill out the curriculum mapping tool, as modeled below. Indicate the mastery level at the end of the week so you can go back in and plan for spiraling/ reteaching as necessary.

Monthly Curriculum Map

	WEEK 1	WEEK 2	WEEK 3	WEEK 4	WEEK 5
READING Mastery Level:	Main Idea and Details	Key ideas			
MATH Mastery Level:	5 digit addition	5 digit subtraction			
SCIENCE Mastery Level:					
SOCIAL STUDIES Mastery Level:					
WRITING Mastery Level:					

Student-Centered Teaching
○ Effect Size of 0.54

As the name indicates, student-centered teaching involves teaching practices that are focused on student engagement. This ensures that our instructional practices revolve around learning experiences that students can relate to. A plethora of research shows the importance of providing engaging, collaborative lessons. When kids work together in small groups or in teams, they have a better chance of retaining the information that is being taught. In a student-centered classroom, you will see students working with other students to figure out concepts and build on their learning.

▦ Procedure

1. After you have planned out your lesson, look at the activities that you have in place for review or practice.

2. Determine a time in the lesson when you can have students work together in collaborative teams to reinforce important concepts.

3. Let students know what the expectations are for their collaborative time.

4. As students are working on their team project, walk around and monitor their progress.

5. Have a set of questions to ask students as they work in groups to help keep the focus. You can ask the following questions:

   • What is your objective?

   • What are your next steps?

   • How can you make your team time more focused?

HELPFUL HINT Student-centered teaching practices are not appropriate for every instructional task. As we noted earlier in this chapter, sometimes direct instruction is an appropriate strategy to use. I have found that student-centered learning lends itself best when students are practicing their learning or are working on end-of-unit projects. Keep in mind that if you are introducing a concept, using a student-centered approach would not be most appropriate because students will need to practice along with the teacher before they can be released to practice with their classmates. Another tip is to make sure that you set clear expectations with your students before releasing them to work in groups.

✎ Reflection

What does student-centered learning mean to you?

_____

_____

_____

For what subjects do you think that a student-centered approach will be most appropriate?

_____

_____

_____

What expectations do you think are most important to focus on before your students work in teams?

_____

_____

_____

📖 Resource

Use these prompts to help plan for student-centered learning.

Lesson objective:

_____

_____

Direct instruction plan:

_____

_____

Student-centered learning activity:

_____

_____

Monitoring of student centered activity:

_____

_____

CHAPTER 7

Implementing Visible Learning in Your Management System

A well-managed classroom is essential for students to achieve high levels of learning. When students do not feel safe and secure in their learning environment, you may see a decline in their learning and achievement.

This chapter focuses on the five factors that are essential to establishing a well-managed classroom: expectation, classroom behavior, classroom management, not labeling students, and reducing anxiety. We will talk about establishing clear rules and expectations for learning, having a strong behavioral plan, and helping students reduce their anxiety by using strategies to help with their well-being. You may be surprised at how having preconceived ideas about your students, and in turn, labeling them, can affect their achievement.

This chapter will also provide some reflection exercises you can use to monitor your management plan and think about ways to strengthen it. I find, as a school principal, that management is essential to providing a learning environment that is conducive to learning and high expectations. When classrooms have well-defined rules and logical consequences for student behavior, learning occurs at much higher rates. On the other hand, when classrooms have poor management guidelines and loose expectations, learning declines. It is a natural occurrence that I have witnessed over and over again. That is why educators spend so much time at the beginning of the year establishing those learning and management routines, so we can start the business of teaching right away.

Behavioral Expectation
○ Effect Size of 0.43

When it comes to behavior, we get what we expect. Expectations are a strong indicator of the type of behaviors that our students will exhibit. According to Hattie's analysis, expectation has a positive effect of 0.43, which would equate to a year of growth. Hattie's study looked at teachers setting high expectations for student learning and academic success; however, I am including this item in the management chapter, because we know that when we have high expectations for student behavior, students rise to the occasion. Expectations can be set for classroom rules, including information about voice level, interaction with others, and other traits.

⊞ Procedure

1. Reinforcing expectations requires that you talk to student about what high expectations mean. Have a discussion with your class about expectations and how they can affect our outcome.

2. Ask students if they have ever thought about something positive happening, and then it did. Let students know that their positive expectations helped them take the steps to fulfill that outcome.

3. If your students don't have any examples, you can share a few personal examples. There are also a lot of success stories online that you can share.

4. Let students know that expectations about our learning and behavior can help us fulfill our desired outcome.

5. Talk to students about what your positive behavior expectations are for them and have them commit to working toward fulfilling those expectations. Let them know you will revisit the criteria as necessary throughout the school year.

HELPFUL HINT Expectation is such an abstract idea, and is something that you are going to have to monitor in yourself. It is not easy to maintain high expectations when current data or behaviors are less than ideal. The trick is to be cognizant of this and to make it a personal commitment to work on your expectations for all students. Kids have good and bad days, and so do we. Take time to look for those bright spots, and to reinforce those positive aspects in your students. As you focus more on the good, you will see more positive behavior and learning in your classroom. Trust me, this works, but it does take a mind shift on your part.

✎ Reflection

Are you a person who sees the glass half full or half empty?

_____

_____

When was a time that you felt very positive?

_____

_____

_____

When was a time that you felt very negative?

_____

_____

_____

How did you maintain that positive place?

_____

_____

_____

How did you work your way out of that negative place?

_____

_____

_____

Which students in your class need to work on having higher expectations for their behavior?

_____

_____

_____

How will you introduce this idea of high expectations to your class and to the students that really need to work on this?

_____

_____

_____

Introduce the concept and come back and journal about what went well and what you need to work on.

_____

_____

_____

After a week of reinforcement, come back and journal about the positive changes you see and the things that still need more practice.

_____

_____

_____

📖 Resource

Distribute this sheet to students, along with the following instructions, as a way to set and reinforce high behavioral expectations.

Use this sheet to track your behavior. A thumbs up means that you were able to be successful in displaying positive behaviors and interactions during this time, with 0 to 2 reminders.

A thumbs down means you needed additional support during this time and received 3 or more reminders. Do your best to get a thumbs up!

	THUMBS UP	THUMBS DOWN
Start of the Day		
Morning Lessons		
Lunch		
Specials		
Afternoon Lessons		
End of the Day		

Classroom Behavior ☉ Effect Size of 0.68

We have known for a long time that classroom management is essential for student learning. If our rooms are out of control, student learning does not occur. Interestingly, Hattie found that when classroom behavior is reinforced and kids receive feedback, we can see a year of growth in achievement. Reinforcement and feedback are highly effective strategies for decreasing classroom behavioral disruptions. This ties into our discussion on expectations: We need to reinforce the behaviors we want students to continue exhibiting and provide immediate feedback on what kids are doing well and what they need to work on. This is more than setting expectations; it is monitoring and supporting those expectations. When students know what the expected positive behavior is in the classroom, playground, or cafeteria, they are more successful.

⊞ Procedure

1. Start by developing a classroom management plan for your class. This plan should include specific and concrete statements about what desired behaviors look like.

2. Your plan should include structures for working alone, in groups, and on non-academic tasks such as going to the restroom, eating in the cafeteria, and playing on the playground.

3. Schools that have a schoolwide plan for conduct have great success, because the skills are expected in all areas and reinforcement is consistent.

4. If your school does not have a schoolwide plan, talk with your administrator about the research and how this may be something worthwhile for your staff to put in place.

5. If your students go to specials and other classrooms throughout the day, share your expectations with the other teachers so they can help reinforce the skills.

6. Teach the behavioral expectations to your students as you would any lesson. Be explicit and provide examples and non-examples.

7. Assess students on their learning by providing scenarios and/or short quizzes.

8. Teaching behavior is like teaching any other skill. You have to scaffold for those that need more support. You can use those students who already have the skills as helpers to assist with reinforcement.

9. Revisit the skills as necessary when you see students need a refresher.

10. Have kids rate their own understanding of the behavioral expectations as a way to hold them accountable for their learning.

HELPFUL HINT Teaching behavioral expectations requires that you remember behaviors are learned and many students have to unlearn some negative behaviors. After long breaks and sometimes weekends, you may find it necessary to reteach skills. Many teachers complain that teaching behavior is a waste of instructional time. However, from Hattie's analysis, we see that not teaching behavior can be detrimental to the learning process. Thus, taking the time to teach behavior will save you a lot of stress and heartache in the future.

✎ Reflection

List the areas in your room where you have found students misbehave. If you have areas in your room that are not supervised, rearrange your environment.

_____

_____

_____

Think about times of the day when your kids have a tendency to need more behavioral support. List these times and think of lessons you can teach to reinforce the desired behavior.

_____

_____

_____

Think about activities when your kids tend to need more behavior support. Create lessons to support students during these activities.

_____

_____

_____

Reflect on a behavior you have taught and how the lesson went. Reflect on what went well and what you need to do as a next step.

_____

_____

_____

📖 Resource

Use the following prompts to track any behavioral infraction hotspots and times of day.

Time(s) of the day with behavioral infractions:

_____

_____

What is happening during this time?

_____

_____

_____

Area(s) in the room with behavioral infractions:

_____

_____

_____

What is helping to contribute to the problems happening in this area?

_____

_____

_____

Student groupings with behavioral infractions:

_____

_____

_____

How are student interactions causing misbehavior?

_____

_____

_____

How can you move kids around to decrease these behaviors?

_____

_____

_____

Down time with behavioral infractions:

_____

_____

_____

Are there times when kids are left unsupervised or without structure?

_____

_____

_____

How can you add structure during these times or have work for them to do?

_____

_____

_____

Transitions with behavioral infractions:

_____

_____

_____

What is happening at the end of your line?

_____

_____

_____

What is happening in the middle of your line?

_____

_____

_____

How are your students behaving as they round corners?

_____

_____

_____

How can you monitor this or put a system in place so there are eyes where you are not?

_____

_____

_____

Classroom Management
○ Effect Size of 0.52

With a positive effect size of 0.52, classroom management is a pivotal tool to increase student achievement. We know that classroom management is important and that we have to have well-managed classrooms in order to teach the content. But, as Hattie often notes, we already know what works—it is just to what extent things work that is important.

Classroom management requires that you, as the teacher, have a set of rules, procedures, and expectations for student learning. It also refers to the systems you have in place to manage materials and transitions in your room. The worst thing is to waste time finding materials for a lesson, only to find that they lead your students to misbehavior. This chain effect is often the result of poor planning. Effective classroom management starts with teacher preparation and planning for all situations that may arise.

⊞ Procedure

1. Develop a classroom management plan for your year. Start by identifying the physical areas in your classroom that require expectations for behavior. For example, how should students behave when sitting at their desks versus in the reading area or when standing up for an activity?

2. List the types of behavior that you want to see in the designated areas and develop a set of expectations for the desired behaviors. When developing expectations, be very explicit about what you want to see and hear.

3. Repeat this process for all of the areas you identified in step 1.

4. Next, think about procedures that are important in your classroom. Procedures may include how to ask to go to the restroom, how to sharpen a pencil, how to turn in homework, and more.

5. Think about the top procedures you want to reinforce for you classroom. Write out clear expectations for these procedures. Include the minute details so your expectations are clearly defined.

6. Write out the details for the procedures. Again, make sure the details are explicit and clear.

7. Repeat the process for the remaining procedures.

8. Finally, develop a list of three to five classroom rules. Some teachers like to develop their rules with their students.

9. If you have a schoolwide plan, incorporate those rules into your classroom procedures planning, but if you are creating your own classroom plans, keep the rules short and written in the positive. For example, you would not write "No hitting," but would instead frame this rule positively: "Keep your hands and feet to yourself."

10. Once your class has agreed to the rules, keep them in a prominent place in the classroom and refer to them frequently.

✎ Reflection

Write about your philosophy on classroom management.

_____

_____

_____

What behaviors cause you stress, or just plain drive you crazy?

_____

_____

_____

What times of the day do your kids need the most redirection?

_____

_____

_____

What are some of the ways you have created your classroom rules in the past?

_____

_____

_____

HELPFUL HINT Developing a positive management system is extremely important. Take the time to really think about the procedures and systems you want to employ in your classroom. Get it right the first time, because you don't want to have to reteach a structure or procedure. It may seem monotonous to write out each and every procedure, but if you take this step it will save you so much time in the long run. I find that when I take that extra 30 to 40 minutes to really think it through, I am clear in my intentions, and in turn, my students are clear of the expectations. Additionally, I find that having the kids help create the rules gives them more ownership and responsibility. I would suggest taking this approach to making your actual classroom rules. Have a set of rules in mind and lead the kids in that direction.

What was successful, and what did not work as well?

_____

_____

_____

How will you ensure that you revisit your classroom rules?

_____

_____

_____

Why are classroom rules important?

_____

_____

_____

Why is it important for you to have procedures in place?

_____

_____

_____

📖 Resource

Use the following tool to come up with a classroom management contract with your class. After your class answers the four questions below, develop a classroom contract to display in your room.

1. What do we, as a class, believe about behavior?

2. What behavior do we agree is not acceptable?

3. What behaviors do we want to foster in our classroom?

4. How will we self-monitor our progress on establishing our desired classroom environment?

Our Classroom Contract

We, the students in room _____, hereby agree to _____

_____

_____.

We will establish a classroom that _____

_____

_____

_____.

Our classroom only _____

_____

_____

_____.

Instead of doing _____

_____

_____,

we _____

_____

_____.

We agree to this contract on the _____ day of _____
in the year _____.

Signatures of all classmates:

Not Labeling Students
○ Effect Size of 0.61

Labeling students is not a positive practice, but we have all been guilty of it. Hattie's study indicates that negative labels can affect student outcomes. We are not just talking about formal labels; we're also talking about labels like "hyper," "bad math student," or "poor reader." Though these labels are not official in any account, our beliefs transfer into our interactions with students and their families.

Not labeling students has a positive effect size of 0.61, which is astonishing. This indicates we can actually propel students forward by not labeling them as incapable of learning. Labeling has a lot to do with mindset and how we transfer mindset to our kids. If a student thinks they cannot do something, they often will not do it. Similarly, if we, as teachers, think a student cannot do something, they often will not. Removing negative labels can work to improve student outcomes by taking away negative stigmas and allowing them to work up to a desired level.

▦ Procedure

1. Where do we start with not labeling students? It begins by determining which labels we have for students that are negative. Take the time to look at your class list and determine what labels you have for students. Be brutally honest. No one is going to see this list; it is for your eyes only.

2. Removing the labels requires placing a new positive label on the student. List each student's positive attributes. For example, if you feel that a student is stubborn, reframe the label to "this student knows themselves well."

3. Think about how these traits can help your students in the future. This will take practice.

4. Once you have identified the negative labels and turned them around to be positive, start to think of ways you can help your students hone in on their strengths. Often, our negative traits can be turned around and made positive. They are often the traits that will make us most productive in life.

5. Teach a lesson on traits and talk about how our strengths might also be some of our more challenging characteristics. Keep the lesson positive: You do not want to polarize students and make them feel bad in any way about their traits. Your job is to find the positive and reinforce it.

HELPFUL HINT Labeling is something we often do subconsciously and it is often difficult to turn a negative into a positive. This will take time and practice. I often start by looking at my own behaviors. I have a tendency to be bossy. I turn this around by noting that I am able to manage others. So, I work on ways to manage in a way that is conducive to teamwork. Try doing the same with your students. Once you are able to notice what their traits are, you will be more capable of turning them around to the positive.

✎ Reflection

List your negative traits and turn them around to positives.

_____

_____

_____

Was that activity difficult to complete? Why or why not?

_____

_____

_____

Choose one student in your classroom and do the same exercise.

_____

_____

_____

Brainstorm a list of positive attributes that you want your students to exhibit.

_____

_____

_____

Who are some characters, in fiction or real life, that exhibit those characteristics?

_____

_____

_____

Brainstorm some ways you can build a connection for your students to the characters and individuals you listed.

_____

_____

_____

📖 Resource

Use the following sheet to list positive behavior traits about each of your students. See the examples to get you started.

STUDENT NAME	POSITIVE TRAITS	HOW WILL THIS HELP OUR CLASS?
Junior James	Likes to share ideas	Can participate in and lead discussions
Sarah Friendly	Is interested in others	Can serve as a buddy for students who are shy or transiting to the classroom
John Cousins	Has a lot of energy	Can help lead games and energizers

STUDENT NAME	POSITIVE TRAITS	HOW WILL THIS HELP OUR CLASS?

Reducing Anxiety ⏺ Effect Size of 0.40

Student learning can be difficult when students feel anxious. Anxiety often occurs when students feel pressured to perform. There are many strategies that you can employ to reduce student anxiety. The most effective way is to create a safe learning environment where students are free to make mistakes without judgment. I am not advocating for lowering your standards; instead, I advocate for creating an environment where students take risks and know they can learn from their mistakes. We learn more from failure than we do from success. The key is to have your students understand this truth.

⊞ Procedure

1. Take an informal assessment of the feel of your classroom. Because you are in your room daily, you are most likely unaware of the vibe in your room. Ask a trusted colleague to sit in and give you an honest assessment.

2. Take your colleague's feedback without rendering any judgment; at the same time, try to find an impartial judge. You don't want someone to tell you all is good when it is not, and you don't want someone to criticize you without looking at all sides. Be strategic in choosing the person you ask to assess your room. You want someone with an objective point of view.

3. After your colleague provides their report, study it and determine what you can do to enhance your environment to make it a risk-free learning zone.

4. Start by thinking of a lesson plan or teachable moment you can use to show students that we all make mistakes and can learn from them. For example, intentionally make your own mistakes and talk about how you bounce back from them.

5. When you see a student taking a risk in their learning, make a big deal of it and celebrate their bravery. Provide incentives for students to take risks; you can offer extra credit for students to do a speech or create a project. Be very intentional and structured in your activities to promote risk taking.

6. Talk to students about anxiety and let them know that we all feel anxious at times. Discuss how your classroom is a safe zone and that they are free to explore their learning without judgment.

7. When you notice kids are feeling anxious, provide time for them to reflect and decompress. You can have a buddy classroom for them to go to in order to calm down, and then have them rejoin the class without incident.

8. As you focus on creating a safe, risk-free environment, you will find that student anxiety levels will decrease.

✎ Reflection

Write about a time when you felt anxious and had to learn something. What was the outcome?

_____

_____

_____

List students in your classroom who have exhibited signs of anxiety.

_____

_____

_____

Commit to finding ways to connect to these students. Write about your interaction.

_____

_____

_____

After a few weeks of building your safe learning zone, write about the subtle changes you have observed.

_____

_____

_____

HELPFUL HINT Creating a risk-free learning zone requires intentional work and continued assessment of your learning environment. Allow your students to take surveys about the learning environment. Students are brutally honest and will let you know if they feel anxiety in the classroom. If you have a school psychologist, talk to them about stress-reducing strategies you can share with your class. They may also be willing to come in to teach those strategies to your class, which is a real win.

📖 Resource

Students can answer these prompts after they've returned from a cool-down area or buddy classroom. Add images or space for drawing to make the prompts more student-friendly.

Draw or write about how you are feeling.

_____

_____

_____

How can you control your emotions better next time?

_____

_____

_____

What will you do next time to be successful?

_____

_____

_____

CHAPTER 8

Implementing Visible Learning in Your Literacy Program

Many techniques and strategies are used to teach literacy, and as a former Title I reading specialist, I have taught or observed them all. I have been in education since the '80s, so I witnessed the reading wars, and I was a child in the '70s when whole language was in full force. I was a proficient reader by the time I was 3 years old, so I've always been drawn to finding ways to help my students learn to read and love it as much as I did as a child. This chapter will provide some exciting information about what works when teaching reading.

A key takeaway of Hattie's visible learning research is that it takes the guesswork out of what works in teaching literacy and provides strategies you can perfect to enhance student learning. The seven strategies you will learn about in this chapter are small group learning, writing programs, phonics instruction, concept mapping, comprehension programs, vocabulary programs, and repeated reading programs. You will uncover how each of these teaching techniques can be implemented in the classroom.

The strategies in this chapter are not intended to be a checklist, or even an exhaustive list, of what works in teaching reading. These are merely the highest leverage strategies in teaching literacy, according to Hattie's meta-analysis. As with any teaching method, if it is not taught with fidelity and if you are not monitoring student progress, results may vary. I can attest to these strategies, as they are all ones that I used as a teacher, with great success.

Small Group Learning ○ Effect Size of 0.49

Small group learning in literacy refers to meeting with groups of students who have similar instructional needs to work on skills and strategies. Research studies have shown that small group learning produces favorable results as a way to improve reading decoding, comprehension, and vocabulary. It has an amazing 0.49 positive effect size. Teaching reading to small groups is often seen in K–2 classrooms, but it is an effective strategy for kids in all grade levels. The area of focus will change depending on the grade level.

⊞ Procedure

1. When planning for small group instruction, the first step is to determine what reading skill or strategy you want to focus on during your teaching. Consider student roles and objectives based on the skill being taught. Decide on the topic that you want your students to work on together, such as story writing or reading from the same book.

2. Think of three to four talking points for your students to cover during their group learning. These points should focus on the most important curricular focus of the standard being taught (for example, the main idea of a passage or a key detail in a text).

3. Share your ground rules for interaction during the group learning. These ground rules may include listening to a classmate's point of view and repeating their thought before building on the discussion.

4. Proceed with the activity and encourage group discussion.

5. Always end the small group session by sharing the key thoughts and ideas that surfaced from the discussion.

HELPFUL HINT   Planning for a small group is not an easy order. Teachers often find this is one of the biggest deterrents from implementing small group instruction during reading. The problem often lies in finding meaningful work for the rest of the class while the teacher meets with small groups. However, with its 0.49 positive effect size, finding ways to make small groups happen is important. Assigning independent work for students not working in small groups helped me run my small groups effectively. See worksheet below.

Another tip is to always read any text before you meet with kids, and script out the questions that you are going to ask. It is not effective to wing it for these groups. Planning for your group time will ensure that you get the positive returns you are expecting.

Reflection

What are the four to five learning centers you will implement?

_____

_____

_____

How will you work to ensure that students who are in the centers are able to work independently?

_____

_____

_____

What can you do to keep kids from interrupting your small group time?

_____

_____

_____

Will you work on skills, strategies, or both during your small reading group?

_____

_____

_____

How will you group kids for small groups?

_____

_____

_____

What assessment tool will you use to group your students?

_____

_____

_____

📖 Resource

Use the chart on page 98 to plan for independent learning centers while you conduct small group learning sessions. These small group learning centers include the Big 5 of reading instruction as identified by the National Reading Panel. I added in writing, as this is an important way for students to share their understanding.

Independent Learning Center Planning

	STUDENTS	FOCUS	OBSERVATION
PHONICS/PHONEMIC AWARENESS			
FLUENCY			
VOCABULARY			
WRITING			
READING COMPREHENSION			

Writing Programs ○ Effect Size of 0.44

Writing programs provide teachers with the opportunity to share their thinking so that it comes alive for students. This is called metacognition or thinking about thinking. This involves the teacher thinking aloud about the thoughts that occur when completing a writing task. I have seen this done with teachers being overly dramatic about how they are coming up with the next thought/idea for their writing piece.

Teachers that model all of these thinking processes provide necessary learning strategies that students will use throughout their academic career to build success.

▦ Procedure

1. Before your writing task, let the students know that you will be modeling for them by thinking aloud.

2. Begin by going through your brainstorm on where you will start with your writing piece.

3. Write your beginning sentences, verbalizing aloud the reason you are writing what you are in the sequence that you are following.

4. As you embark on the next stage of the writing process, again verbalize your thinking.

5. Continue this process until the writing task has been completed.

6. Inquire if students have any questions regarding your writing process.

7. As you answer student questions, ensure that you go back to your thinking process and how it allowed you to come up with your actions.

HELPFUL HINT   Always practice writing the piece before the lesson. As you do so, have a sheet of paper where you can write down the thought process that you followed to complete the task. This may seem odd because as a fluent writer, you write without thinking. You want to slow it down, however, and note your own thinking so you can share it with your students.

✎ Reflection

Do you feel anxious about modeling your thinking? Why?

_____

_____

_____

What would be a benefit of bringing your thinking to the forefront in your lesson? Why is this important in writing?

_____

_____

_____

Commit to presenting at least one metacognitive writing lesson in the next week. After you compete the lesson, reflect on your experience.

_____

_____

_____

📖 Resource

Answer the following prompts to plan for writing instruction.

Unit: _____

Standard: _____

Writing concept to be modeled:

_____

_____

Teacher input:

_____

_____

Student guided practice:

_____

_____

Student independent practice:

_____

_____

Assessment:

_____

_____

Phonics Instruction ☿ Effect Size of 0.54

A few decades ago, the National Reading Panel concluded that phonics instruction was pivotal to student success in reading. Phonics instruction refers to explicit instruction in phonics for students. This instruction involves teaching the overarching principles of phonemic awareness, or sound and oral correspondence; and phonics, the connection between letters and sounds, and the connection between written symbols and sounds. For phonics instruction to be effective, it must follow a prescribed sequence so that students can practice in isolation and with text to solidify their learning.

▦ Procedure

1. Decide on the phonics activity you want to teach.

2. Make sure your lesson is systematic and organized. Ensure that the lesson follows a deliberate sequence. This should include guided practice, independent practice, and a conclusion or assessment.

3. Build on what the students know in your phonics lesson. This allows students to solidify their learning and increases fluency.

4. Provide multiple opportunities for students to apply the new learning in context. Allow them to read and write using the phonics skill that was taught.

When teaching phonics, it is important to follow the developmental progression for phonics acquisition. The progressions are typically as follows:

Kindergarten	1st Grade	2nd Grade	3rd Grade
Sound correspondence	Sound combinations, including digraphs	Sound knowledge of diphthongs and digraphs	Sound knowledge of more advanced diphthongs and digraphs
Decoding of one-syllable words	Decoding with increased automaticity	Decoding, including compound words	Decoding of more complex words, including those with inflectional endings and contractions
Basic sight reading	Sight reading	Sight reading	Sight reading with accuracy and fluency

If you have access to a basal reading program, I would follow the sequence in the basal series for a systematic method of instruction.

I would also suggest you talk with the teachers in the grade levels before you to see where they end in their phonics instruction so you have continuity in your program.

✎ Reflection

Why is teaching phonics important?

_____

_____

_____

How can having a knowledge of phonics helps students in their reading?

_____

_____

_____

Read the National Reading Panel research on teaching reading (see Literacy resources on page 178), and write about your learning.

_____

_____

_____

How will you incorporate phonics instruction into your teaching this week?

_____

_____

_____

Phonics Lesson Planning Sheet

CONCEPT	
LEARNING OBJECTIVE	
TEACHING Create a direct instruction lesson plan.	
PRACTICE AND APPLICATION Activities for the whole group and for independent work.	
ASSESSMENT Assess student knowledge of the phonics concept.	
REFLECTION What went well? What are the next steps?	

Concept Mapping ○ Effect Size of 0.49

Concept mapping involves creating a graphic representation of the concepts that are being taught. It is most effective when students are involved in the development of the graphic. Concept maps provide an opportunity for students to group attributes according to criteria. This allows students to synthesize their learning and visualize the connections. Unlike common graphic organizers, a concept map is also called a visual map because of the ideas it supports. These include pattern recognition, identifying key concepts, and identifying context.

▦ Procedure

1. Concept mapping typically starts with a question. Pose the question to your class. For example: What is a mammal? Who lives in Antarctica?

2. Place the question in the center of the map.

3. Have the students help fill out the terms that belong in the chain.

4. Have the students come up with subcategories that connect to the main concept.

5. As a class, fill out those areas on the map.

6. Continue the process until the map is complete.

HELPFUL HINT   Have questions in mind before you share the concept map with your class. This will help ensure you have a map that students will be able to successfully fill out. Determine what some secondary categories might be in your concept map. Be prepared to share these with students if they are not able to come up with them on their own.

✎ Reflection

Why are concept maps a great way to teach to mastery?

_____

_____

_____

How can you use concept maps to teach literacy standards?

_____

_____

_____

Think about upcoming lessons and how you can incorporate concept maps in your teaching.

_____

_____

_____

📖 Resource

Here's an example of a concept map that you can use in your classroom to discuss whales.

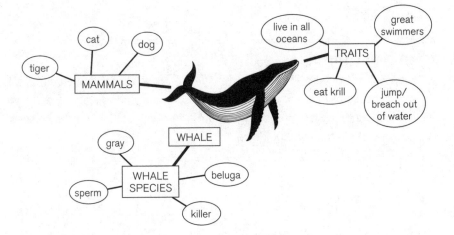

Comprehension Programs
⟳ Effect Size of 0.60

The ultimate goal of reading is comprehension. Often teachers assume that their students understand how to comprehend fiction and non-fiction text. However, research shows that students need explicit instruction in comprehension. Comprehension programs focus on the key components of reading comprehension, which include making predictions, making inferences, drawing conclusions, comparing and contrasting, finding the main idea, making connections, interpreting graphics, evaluating facts and opinions, and summarizing. As you can see, there are a lot of skills that encompass comprehension, thus comprehension programs are essential to ensure students master these necessary skills. With a positive effect size of 0.60, having a systematic comprehension program is important.

▦ Procedure

1. When looking for an effective comprehension program, you want to make sure the program teaches all of the key components of comprehension, including phonics, fluency, vocabulary, and written expression.

2. It is important to find a program that teaches comprehension strategies for fiction and non-fiction text, as the text structure of each is very distinct.

3. When teaching the comprehension strategy, use your metacognitive strategies to help students internalize the process they should follow to comprehend text.

4. Teach using explanations, demonstrations, metacognitive examples, and practice.

5. Have students apply the strategies in context.

6. Use anchor charts in the classroom so students can access the strategies that have been taught.

HELPFUL HINT   We often assume that students know that the purpose of reading is to comprehend text. The fact is, many students are struggling with decoding, so comprehension is not what they are focusing on. That is why teaching students to read with fluency is so important.

Comprehension programs should place students in authentic reading and writing activities. The key is to teach comprehension strategies with precision so that students can have a toolbox of strategies they can use when reading. When teaching reading comprehension strategies, tie them into writing so that students can transfer their learning. Remember, students don't learn to comprehend by simply reading a lot of text. These strategies must be taught explicitly and in context so students can internalize the concepts and master them.

✎ Reflection

Why should we teach comprehension?

_____

_____

_____

How can writing help students with their comprehension?

_____

_____

_____

Write about a way you will teach comprehension this week.

_____

_____

_____

After your lesson, reflect below on how the lesson went and what you will do next time to make it better.

_____

_____

_____

📖 Resource

Use this worksheet to plan your comprehension strategies.

Sequencing

FIRST	NEXT	THEN

Rereading

Read the text.

Do you understand what you just read?

Reread if you did not understand the meaning of what was read.

Visualization

What do you see?

What can you hear?

What can you smell?

What would it taste like?

What might it feel like?

Making connections

How is this text like something you've read before?

How is this text like something you've experienced in your own life?

Determining importance

What is most important about what you just read?

What was the text mainly about?

What is important to remember?

Vocabulary Programs ○ Effect Size of 0.67

With such a high effect size, it is important to think about the implications of having a large vocabulary. Students with a strong vocabulary have a better chance of comprehending text. They don't have to expend energy trying to figure out what words mean, but are able to read fluently and comprehend what they are reading. They also have an easier time responding to questions and are able to articulate their ideas fluently in both speaking and writing.

There are many vocabulary programs available, but when looking for a program, be sure that the one you choose has explicit instruction that builds on the key strategies to figure out unknown words. These strategies include context clues, Frayer model, and word analysis. When you use context clues, you teach students to look at the surrounding text to figure out unknown words. The Frayer model provides a graphic organizer that helps students think about a word and provide a definition, example, non-example, and characteristics of a vocabulary word. This allows students to get to know the word at deeper levels. Finally, word analysis requires students to look at the parts of words (like the prefix and suffix) to help determine the meaning of the word. This is especially important as students get into higher levels of school and encounter words rooted in Latin.

▦ Procedure

1. When looking for an effective vocabulary program, you want to ensure the program teaches the key components of vocabulary instruction. Find a program that immerses students in words through listening, speaking, reading, and writing.

2. Scaffold the learning by revisiting key words.

3. Incorporate programs that teach strategies for figuring out unknown words and that teach word parts.

4. When teaching the vocabulary lesson, be sure to teach the vocabulary words in context so students can transfer the learning.

5. Use word-study activities like word sorts and word maps to deepen their comprehension.

If you do not have a scripted program and are working on vocabulary on your own, there are few things to keep in mind. First, be sure to start by defining the word for kids. Make sure that your definition is kid friendly. Provide a picture that represents the word so kids have a visual representation of the word. Vocabulary is typically revisited throughout the week, so each day, build on student knowledge of the word by having them draw, write about, and discuss the vocabulary words. This will help to solidify the meaning.

✎ Reflection

What are some key vocabulary words your students need to learn at your grade level?

_____

_____

_____

What are some vocabulary games you can implement in your classroom?

_____

_____

_____

In an upcoming unit, pick 10 key vocabulary words that you will teach.

_____

_____

_____

📖 Resource

Use the following worksheet to teach new vocabulary words.

Word:_____

Definition:

_____

_____

HELPFUL HINT Vocabulary instruction doesn't have to be boring. You can liven it up by having students act out their vocabulary words, draw pictures, or write sentences about the words they acquire. Your goal is to build a love of words in your students so they find it fun to learn and build their vocabulary.

Visual representation:

_____

_____

What is the opposite of the word?

_____

_____

Use in a sentence:

_____

_____

_____

_____

Repeated Reading Programs ○ Effect Size of 0.67

Repeated reading programs are used to build fluency and comprehension in reading. They typically involve reading a passage repeatedly until the student can read it with fluency. This strategy came into popularity in the '80s, when many schools started testing on short fluency passages to assess reading. When implementing these programs, make sure the passages are at the students' reading ability level. You want them to build up to reading grade level texts with accuracy.

⊞ Procedure

1. When looking for a repeated reading program you want to ensure the program builds on students' reading levels. You also want a program that allows students to read both fiction and non-fiction text.

2. Comprehension testing should be a key component of the program selected. Students need to be assessed on the text they read so they understand the importance of comprehending their text.

3. If you are teaching repeated reading on your own, pick a passage that is between 50 and 100 words.

4. Select text that has decodable words, frequently found vocabulary words, and popular phrases.

5. Read the passage aloud to the student and have them follow along.

6. Have the student read the passage aloud repeatedly until they can read it fluently.

HELPFUL HINT Repeated reading is a high-impact strategy that can easily be implemented into your teaching. If you find that you cannot read with the student directly, you can record yourself reading the passage, have the student listen to the text, and then have them record themselves until they can read it with fluency. You can then listen to the recordings when you have time so you can assess their fluency progress.

✎ Reflection

How will repeated reading help your students with their fluency and comprehension?

_____

_____

_____

What are some ways you can implement repeated reading during your reading block?

_____

_____

_____

How could repeated reading look if it were turned into a learning center?

_____

_____

_____

📖 Resource

Use these prompts to help plan for your implementation of repeated reading. At the end of the teaching, have students summarize the text. This helps them internalize the importance of reading as a way to comprehend meaning.

Text:_____

Lexile level: _____

Genre: _____

Vocabulary words needed for comprehension:

_____

_____

_____

Comprehension questions:

_____

_____

_____

_____

Recall question:

_____

_____

_____

_____

Question on theme or main idea:

_____

_____

_____

_____

CHAPTER 9

Implementing Visible Learning in Your Math Program

When planning for a math lesson, it is important to think about your learners and what teaching strategies and structures will be most impactful for their success. The fact is, we teach a lot like the way we were taught in school. Our math programs in America have often been teacher directed, where students learn a set of concepts and move forward so that the curriculum can be covered. This method of teaching often leaves those students who have not mastered the concepts behind. As they move through school, this shows up as gaps in understanding. I often hear teachers talk about students in middle school and high school who have trouble with fractions or multiplication, which they never mastered in grammar school.

Teaching mathematics requires that teachers concretely understand the math concepts so that they can impart this information to their students. We are often told that teaching math requires students to go beyond the numbers and understand the conceptual level of the math they are learning. For example, students grasp concepts more quickly when they can visualize the meaning, like seeing that one half is represented by breaking a cookie in half or that thirds can be represented by three pieces making a whole pie. When I was taught math in school, we did not use visual models to help make the learning more visible.

Instead, we learned a lot of formulas and solved a lot of practice problems. Math was not necessarily my strongest subject, but I enjoyed it enough to take the time to learn concepts beyond what my teachers shared.

In this chapter, we will cover five strategies to help make your mathematics instruction more visible and impactful for student success. The five concepts covered include mathematics programs, problem solving, questioning, worked examples, and cooperative versus individualistic learning. Each of these strategies will be helpful in providing students with the steps and tools needed to be successful.

Mathematics Programs
○ Effect Size of 0.40

Mathematics programs that are systematic, provide opportunities for students to scaffold their learning, and allow frequent practice are proven to be most effective, with a positive effect size of 0.40. When looking for mathematics programs, it is important to determine the level of interaction supported by the program. Research studies show that math programs that allow for student interaction are more successful than those that do not. It is also important that the programs focus on problem solving and conceptual understanding.

▦ Procedure

1. When planning for math instruction, it is important to determine what standard or skill you want students to practice during the lesson.

2. Once you determine the skill or strategy, map out the steps you will take to present the learning. Build in high-leverage strategies like modeling, think-alouds, and visual representations. Use all of these strategies to make the math program stronger.

3. When modeling, give students time to practice each chunk of the learning before moving on. Don't move too quickly or too slowly on this part. Having that perfect model will help students master the learning.

4. When you employ metacognitive practices, make sure you script out your think-aloud so you hit on the most important details.

5. Ensure that your visual representations provide key vocabulary and steps that students can use to solve the problems. These visual representations should be thought of as a support tool students can access at any time.

HELPFUL HINT   We know that effective mathematics programs have a systematic approach of teaching that includes opportunities for student practice. Practice activities should build on what you are teaching and provide small chunks of learning to help kids build fluency. Start with a problem that you solve together. Then, have students solve a problem using the same format, but with different numbers. Once they show mastery on this format, you can introduce more difficult problems for them to practice.

✎ Reflection

How will you build in conversation during your math lessons?

_____

_____

_____

What are some math concepts your students need practice on?

_____

_____

_____

How will you ensure students have enough time to work on the math skills they need more practice with?

_____

_____

_____

How will you check for understanding and know when to move on when students are working on practice problems?

_____

_____

_____

📖 Resource

Use these sentence starters to aid students in discussion.

I have a question about...

_____

_____

I am wondering...

_____

_____

I disagree because...

_____

_____

My answer is different because...

_____

_____

I agree because...

_____

_____

I think this is true because...

_____

_____

I got the same answer because...

_____

_____

I think...

_____

_____

You could try...

_____

_____

Another way to solve this problem is...

_____

_____

What I am hearing you say is...

_____

_____

You just said…

_____

_____

Problem Solving ○ Effect Size of 0.61

Problem solving involves students finding an issue and working to find solutions to the problem. This technique works well in teaching math and science. Problem solving provides opportunities for students to work collaboratively and use critical thinking skills. It also requires that students use multiple strategies and skills that they have acquired. Problem solving involves higher-level thinking because it requires students to synthesize their learning across different content areas. With a positive effect size of 0.61, including problem solving in your teaching repertoire will be beneficial.

▦ Procedure

1. Think of a problem that needs to be solved using mathematics. It could be a division problem, multiplication problem, or anything else. I suggest making it a problem that revisits a math concept you are working on.

2. Pose the problem to the class and ask them how they think they can solve the problem.

3. Once the class has come up with a strategy (or strategies), have students work in teams to find the solution.

4. As the students work collaboratively to solve the problem, offer guidance as needed.

5. After teams have worked collaboratively, have students work on their solutions independently.

6. Let teams report their solutions to the class.

7. Provide feedback as teams present their solutions, and have the class discuss what they think about the different solutions.

8. Correct student misconceptions as necessary.

9. Discuss how problem solving helped the class approach the problem in varied ways. Emphasize the fact that there was not just one, but multiple solutions to the problem.

HELPFUL HINT   The only way this activity will work is if you provide a problem that has multiple solutions. Take the time to find a problem that can be solved using different math operations. When supporting students, be careful not to give the answer away. Instead, gently guide the students. It will be really important to emphasize that problem solving can be done in different ways and that there is not one correct answer.

✎ Reflection

How will problem solving help your students become more reflective learners?

_____

_____

_____

What is a problem that you can pose to your students?

_____

_____

_____

How will you ensure students have a productive struggle with the problem? Remember, you don't want it to be too easy.

_____

_____

_____

📖 Resource

Students can use these prompts to help them think about problem solving.

Name: _____

The problem is:

_____

_____

One way to solve this problem is to:

_____

_____

Another alternative is to:

_____

_____

Questioning ○ Effect Size of 0.48

Questioning is used to guide student learning in mathematics. The questions that you ask, and the way you ask them, can help students determine the most logical way to solve mathematical problems, guiding students to higher levels of meaning. It stimulates conversation and mathematical thinking. Of course, not all questions are created equal. Teachers must think about the questions they will ask and how their questions will lead students to think and understand mathematical concepts.

🖩 Procedure

1. When planning for your math lesson, think of questions that you want to pose to assess student learning.

2. Write the questions out on sticky notes and place them in your plans or math book so that you don't forget to ask them.

3. Have several questions ready so you can use those that are most necessary for your lesson, depending on how the learning flows.

4. Write questions that are at different levels of difficulty. Start with basic questions that are rote in nature and move up to more complex questions as you progress through the lesson.

5. Finish your lesson with a question you can use to summarize student understanding. Use this question as an assessment piece.

HELPFUL HINT Many teachers are good at posing questions for literature and social studies, but they struggle with questioning in mathematics. Remember to apply the same thinking to the questions that you use when teaching mathematics. Ask questions that will keep your students engaged with the task, and that are relevant and allow students to think outside of the box. Also, listen to your students' responses, as they can help guide your lessons and allow you to make adjustments in your teaching as necessary.

✎ Reflection

How did the questions you wrote challenge your students?

_____

_____

_____

How can you make one of the questions better?

_____

_____

_____

What is an overarching question you can ask to assess student learning at the end of the lesson?

_____

_____

_____

📖 Resource

Planning for Math Questioning Sheet

TYPE	EXAMPLE	QUESTION
Recall and reproduction: recall of facts, definitions, and terms.	Who was the first president of the United States? What planet is closest to Earth? What is the definition of photosynthesis?	
Basic skills and concepts: requires students to make a decision about how to approach and solve a problem.	Interpret information in a chart, or solve a routine math problem.	
Strategic thinking: requires students to explain their thinking.	Explain how to solve a math problem with more than one correct answer, or formulate a problem when given a solution.	
Extended thinking: reasoning over an extended period of time.	Relate math problems to real-world scenarios, or conduct a research project that involves several mathematical problems.	

Worked Examples ○ Effect Size of 0.57

Worked examples provide models of how to complete a mathematical task. They are the examples often found in math textbooks. These examples provide context for students so they can see the thought process and work required to solve a math problem. When I was a math student, I always looked at the worked examples to help clarify any misconceptions I had about a math concept.

Worked examples have a 0.57 positive effect on student learning. That is why they are found in nearly every math textbook you find today. Worked examples should be used to scaffold early learning. However, research suggests that as students grow in their understanding, worked examples should be phased out.

▦ Procedure

1. Decide on a few math problems that students will be learning.

2. On a sheet of paper, work out the problem. Show all of your work on the example.

3. Transfer the work example to a sheet of chart paper to share with your class.

4. When sharing the worked example, talk through your thought process.

5. Provide the students with problems to solve that follow the same sequence as the one shown in worked example.

6. Have students share how the worked example helped them solve the problems with greater fluency.

⫻ **HELPFUL HINT** Remember that worked examples should be used as students are learning new concepts. Worked examples are not as effective with concepts that students have mastered. The problems that students solve should match with the worked example so students can use the example as a model.

Case Study

Michelle taught math in high school and at the college level in Arizona for over five years. Worked examples was a strategy she used to improve student results. Here's her takeaway:

Worked examples are very important in math. For example, when teaching the distributive property in algebra, you can include a worked example that is color coded by each step, along with an explanation for each step. This helps take the pressure off the students. As the teacher, you are easily able to walk them through the steps and explain why you have done each step. Students can concentrate on how each step works together with the next to complete the process, instead of worrying about choosing the right numbers or making sure that they multiply correctly, for example.

✎ Reflection

How can using worked examples help you ensure your students grasp math concepts?

_____

_____

_____

What are a few math concepts that are coming up in your teaching where worked examples may be helpful?

_____

_____

_____

How will these worked examples enhance your students' conception of the strategy or skill?

_____

_____

_____

Cooperative vs. Individualistic Learning ○ Effect Size of 0.50

Mathematics is often taught as an individualistic task, but cooperative practices in learning has a 0.50 positive effect size. Cooperative learning involves having students work in groups as they are learning. This imparts a social aspect to learning that is effective in fostering engagement. Because it provides many opportunities for students to solve problems and discuss their strategies, math is a perfect subject for engaging students in cooperative learning structures.

▦ Procedure

1. Set up your learning environment in a way that is conducive to student interaction.

2. Create problems that involve problem solving and that lend themselves to students working in pairs or teams to solve. Then, give students a set of math problems to solve.

3. As students are solving the problems, provide feedback when necessary.

4. Have students share what their team learned when working together.

5. Ask students what they learned by working with someone else to solve the math problem.

6. Lead students in a discussion about the impact of working with others to solve complex problems.

HELPFUL HINT When having students work in cooperative groups, be sure to set clear parameters for behavior. Often, teachers fail to use cooperative group-ings because of management issues. Curtail these issues by taking the time to set clear expectations for behavior. Cooperative learning in math can be done as a center-time activity. It should not take the place of direct instruction, which also has a high positive effect size.

✎ Reflection

What apprehension, if any, do you have about using cooperative learning during math?

_____

_____

_____

What are your thoughts on using cooperative learning as a center-type activity?

_____

_____

_____

How will you set up your room so it is conducive to cooperative learning?

_____

_____

_____

📖 Resource

Give students these questions as a tool for self-evaluation.

I contributed to the team by...

_____

_____

I shared my knowledge with my team members by...

_____

_____

An example of when I listened to others in my team is...

_____

_____

I supported the efforts of my team by...

_____

_____

One way I will improve my teamwork is...

_____

_____

CHAPTER 10

Implementing Visible Learning Assessment and Grading Practices

Assessment and grading are two of the most important tasks we complete as educators. The term "assessment-driven instruction" has been tossed about in education for decades, but what do we really mean by this? Assessment should be the driver that takes the pulse on how our teaching is going. With properly developed assessments, we can determine if our students are actually learning what we are teaching.

I must admit that assessment is one of my favorite topics in education. As a teacher, I used formal and informal assessments as my way of determining my next steps in teaching. For me, it just didn't make sense to move forward in teaching without assessing. My assessments were not elaborate or time consuming. A quick check after a chunk of the lesson was enough for me to determine where my kids were in relation to the learning.

In this chapter, we will look at five high-leverage strategies to use when assessing students. The strategies we will look at are mastery learning, self-reported grades, response to intervention, feedback, and early interventions. Each of these strategies are useful for advancing learning and determining the instructional focus. This chapter will be one you will want to come back to time and time again as you develop your toolkit of instructional strategies.

Mastery Learning ○ Effect Size of 0.58

Mastery learning refers to teaching all students until they achieve mastery. It is based on Benjamin Bloom's theory of the level of mastery. According to Bloom, students must move up the levels on the taxonomy of learning to reach mastery. Those levels are knowledge, comprehension, application, analysis, synthesis, and evaluation. Evaluation is the highest level and knowledge is the most basic.

Mastery learning depends on assessing students at each level of competency in order to determine how close they are to mastering the skill or concept. Mastery learning is a great leveling tool for students of all academic and social levels, thus its positive effect size of 0.58. However, one caveat to mastery learning is that it requires teachers not move on to another subject or skill until all students have fully grasped the content. This is indeed controversial when we think about all of the standards that need to be taught in one school year. Some teachers have found mastery learning works best in subjects where there is not such huge gap in ability level in their classroom.

▦ Procedure

1. Choose a high-level or foundational standard or skill for your students to master. Remember, not all standards and skills are created

equal. Pick one that will give you more bang for your buck. For example, students will need to know how to compare and contrast in most subjects they encounter. Knowing alphabetical order, although important, is something they can use a dictionary for.

2. Plan your lesson and ensure that you are going up the levels on Bloom's taxonomy.

3. Start by asking general knowledge questions.

4. Teach by application, where the students will use their learning to develop a project.

5. Assess students at each level of teaching and do not move on until students have mastered the skill or standard.

6. Continue the cycle until you have moved to the final level of evaluation.

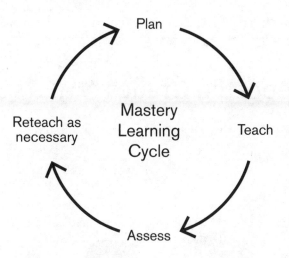

✎ Reflection

Why is mastery teaching important?

_____

_____

_____

How will you slow down your teaching to ensure that all students reach mastery?

_____

_____

_____

What do you think will be most challenging in mastery teaching?

_____

_____

_____

How will you combat this challenge?

_____

_____

_____

Self-Reported Grades ○ Effect Size of 1.44

Self-reported grades is the most effective strategy, according to John Hattie's research. With an impressive positive correlation to student success, it has a positive effect size of 1.44. That is over a year of growth, so taking an in-depth look at this strategy is merited.

When students see that they have control over their learning and that they can determine their outcomes, we see tremendous gains. Self-reported grading asks

HELPFUL HINT Teaching to mastery requires that you know what mastery looks like. Take the time to really understand the skill or standard and use a backward model, planning based on where you want kids to be at the end of your teaching. This means you will move down the levels, starting from evaluation and moving to initial knowledge. This will allow you to fill in any holes when you teach. It is also helpful to run your assessments by a colleague. Tell them the level of mastery you are assessing and get their opinion on the assessment items.

students to assess their own learning and determine where they will fall on an assessment. Research shows that students are very good at predicting their grades, and as they continue in the practice they become even more accurate. Self-reporting teaches kids to think about their own learning, which in turn causes them to signify what they know and do not know. When students are aware of their own deficits, they can target their studying efforts to bridge the gap. This creates self-monitoring, which is the ultimate objective in teaching and learning.

We want students to become self-sufficient, regulated learners who can work to hone in on their learning. Depending on the grade level you teach, the scaffolds you provide for self-reported grading will vary. Students in elementary grades can use rubrics and sample assignments to show what mastery looks like.

▦ Procedure

1. Let students know they will be assessing their own learning and will determine what grade they think their project or test will earn. Note that self-grading does not replace teacher grading and assessments.

2. Start by sharing examples of work and having kids rate what grade they think the project or assignment has earned.

3. Start with obvious examples and move up to complex examples that may not be so explicit.

4. Share the rubric and/or example for the task or assignment that students have completed.

5. Explain what each indicator on the rubric means and/or go over the sample assignment to explain how it will be graded.

6. Ask students to look at their project/assignment and have them assign it a grade.

7. Conference with students individually afterward and let them know how they fell on the formal grading scale.

8. Talk about how their self-reported grades matched or did not match with the final grade.

9. Clear up any misconceptions that the student may have had in their prediction.

10. Continue to practice this skill of self-reporting grades on assignments that are most conducive to this strategy. The goal is for students to internalize this practice and learn to do it instinctively.

11. Have periodic meetings with students to go over their self-assessments and clear up any confusion as necessary.

HELPFUL HINT   Teaching students to self-report their grades shifts the responsibility of learning in the classroom. As you teach students to slow down and look at their progress, you are teaching them an important life skill they will use for many years to come. Some students may be continually off base with their predictions. If this is the case, work with those students individually and assess with them until they are able to see how to look at an assignment and self-assess. Use your metacognitive strategies and think aloud about the process you follow when you self-assess.

✎ Reflection

What are some upcoming opportunities where you can use self-reported grading?

_____

_____

_____

How will you create a rubric that is student friendly?

_____

_____

_____

What do you think will be most challenging in teaching students to self-report their grades?

_____

_____

_____

How will you combat this challenge?

_____

_____

_____

After your students complete one self-grading assignment, use the space below to reflect on the experience.

_____

_____

_____

Response to Intervention
○ Effect Size of 1.07

Response to intervention (RTI) is a system to identify and provide tiers of intervention for students in a multi-tiered system. The tiers are Tier 1, which is the instruction that all students receive no matter their level of achievement; Tier 2, which is targeted small-group instruction for students that are not making progress in Tier 1; and Tier 3, which is individualized instruction that targets deficits and is a system to ensure future problems are curtailed.

RTI has a positive effect size of 1.07. Assessment plays a pivotal part in response to intervention. Districts typically use benchmark assessments to place students in intervention groups. These assessments identify deficits and have progress monitors to determine how students are progressing toward achieving proficiency.

▦ Procedure

1. The RTI model starts with a benchmark assessment to screen students to determine where they fall in their level of proficiency or deficiency. Screenings are used to place students into groups.

2. Most of the scales signify students as intensive (below standard), strategic (lacking some essential skills), and benchmark (meeting proficiency).

3. Students that are strategic, or mid-level, are typically grouped to receive Tier 2 instruction. These groups should be fluid, and assessment should be given at least every other week to determine progress.

4. Students that are intensive should receive targeted Tier 3 intervention in a research-based program that is aligned to the specific deficits of the student. These students will need more time to master deficit skills and build on them.

5. Tier 3 instruction must be not only targeted, but frequent in order to move learning forward. Ideally, assessments should be given weekly for Tier 3 students to track progress.

6. All students, regardless of their level of achievement, will receive Tier 1 instruction, which is instruction that teaches the necessary standards and skills for the grade level.

7. Keep in mind that students often have higher listening comprehension levels than reading levels, and math concepts can be scaffolded to meet the needs of all learners.

_✐_ **HELPFUL HINT** Response to intervention is a system that works best when you have a school-wide plan. Finding targeted intervention programs requires research. Be sure that the intervention matches the level of deficit, and also be sure to provide enough lessons in the intervention before you determine if it works or not.

✎ Reflection

What does the response to intervention program at your school look like?

_____

_____

_____

What does your Tier 1 instruction look like?

_____

_____

_____

What does your Tier 2 instruction look like?

_____

_____

_____

What type of Tier 3 instruction does your school have?

_____

_____

_____

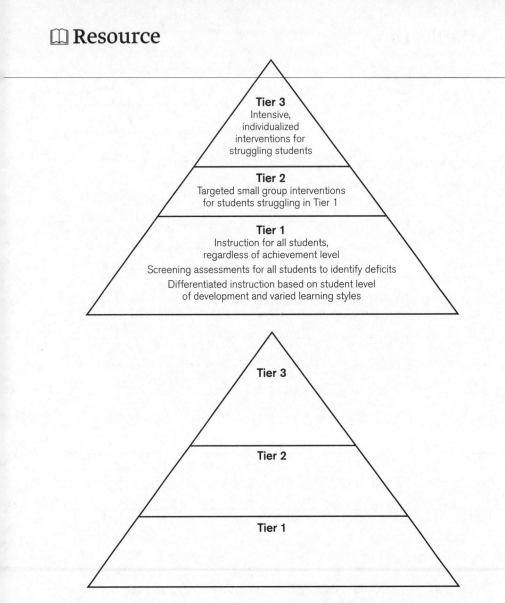

Tier 3
Intensive,
individualized
interventions for
struggling students

Tier 2
Targeted small group interventions
for students struggling in Tier 1

Tier 1
Instruction for all students,
regardless of achievement level
Screening assessments for all students to identify deficits
Differentiated instruction based on student level
of development and varied learning styles

Tier 3

Tier 2

Tier 1

Fill in each section with the instruction that is occurring at each level.

Feedback 🍎 Effect Size of 0.75

Providing feedback to learners is important for student achievement. However, feedback must be specific in order for students to use it to improve in their learning. Teachers often give feedback, but it is general and may be about the learner, not the task. Feedback should not be about how smart a student is or how hard they work. It should instead be about the specific task and what the student did. For example, you can tell a student what steps they took in solving a problem and how those steps helped them get to the correct answer. Feedback also must be given in real time. You want to give feedback as quickly as possible so students can connect it with the activity or action they completed.

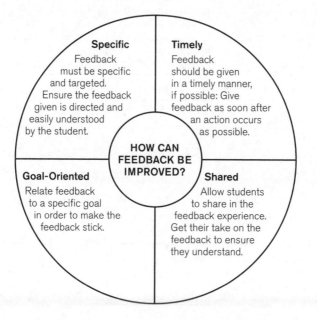

Procedure

1. When you are teaching a lesson, remember to stop to provide specific feedback to students. This might look like stating what behavior or action a student exhibited, and how it helped or hurt the situation.

2. The key is to not focus on giving the student feedback that is personal, but instead, provide feedback that focuses on the task.

3. Practice by writing out specific language you may use to provide targeted feedback.

4. You can also practice with a colleague by having them give you feedback on how specific your feedback is.

✎ Reflection

Write about a time when you received specific feedback. How did it help you grow in your practice?

_____

_____

_____

Why did the feedback you received help you move forward in your learning?

_____

_____

_____

How will providing feedback help your students grow?

_____

_____

_____

What challenges do you think you will encounter in providing specific feedback?

_____

_____

_____

HELPFUL HINT   Providing feedback requires that you stay in the moment while you're teaching. Remember that feedback needs to be specific and in real time; timing is essential. It can be hard to keep up with feedback, so try to make a goal of giving feedback to three students per lesson. As you gain more comfort with giving feedback, it will become more natural.

Early Interventions ⟳ Effect Size of 0.47

We have long known that early intervention is useful for closing the achievement gap. The earlier we can target deficits and intervene, the better chance we have of bridging the gap. Studies have indicated that the older students are, the more time they need for intervention; thus, early intervention is warranted.

Early intervention falls in the assessment chapter because we have to assess student learning to conclude whether they need intervention. Intervention must be based on student need, determined by using a universal screening tool or a well-written common assessment. If we intervene on a whim, we will not be targeting what students need. Instead, it must be targeted and aligned specifically to student need. If we do it any other way, students may receive intervention on a skill they are proficient in, or they may not receive intervention for a deficit, which would be a waste of precious instructional time.

▦ Procedure

1. Assess your students using a benchmark assessment that measures the area of need you want to intervene in. Assessments should be research validated. Your district should have norm-referenced assessments that they use to assess math and reading. Remember, the assessment should be a screening tool that you can use to determine the specific intervention that is needed.

2. Once the assessment data is received, look at the reports or analyze the data yourself and decide the area of deficit you want to focus on with your student.

3. Plan for an intervention that is targeted to the area of need.

4. Make this intervention your priority so you can adhere to early intervention, before the negative learning practices become more cemented in the student.

5. To ensure you have early intervention, you must employ an intervention cycle where you, as the teacher, are continually assessing your students and intervening as necessary.

6. You can develop skills groups made up of students that have like needs as a means of providing targeted intervention.

7. Once students have mastered a skill, move them out of the intervention and move other students in to maintain a flow to your intervention cycle.

HELPFUL HINT You don't want to release students from intervention too soon. The way to avoid this is to assess your students frequently and to have fluid intervention groups. Flexibility allows you to provide balanced intervention, as needed.

Often, we struggle with finding time for intervention, but intervention does not have to be an hour long. You can meet with students for 15 to 20 minutes and provide targeted intervention that will close the achievement gap. The key is to provide intervention that targets the specific needs of the student.

✎ Reflection

Look at your most recent assessment data and write about the student areas of need.

_____

_____

_____

What are the greatest areas of need in reading and math?

_____

_____

_____

How will you target intervention in the greatest areas of need?

_____

_____

_____

How many intervention lessons will you provide?

_____

_____

_____

How will you assess when students are ready to move forward from intervention?

_____

_____

_____

📖 Resource

As you implement interventions, use this sheet to track student progress and determine when students need to move from one intervention to the next.

DATE	INTERVENTION GIVEN	STUDENT(S)	ASSESSMENT RESULTS

DATE	INTERVENTION GIVEN	STUDENT(S)	ASSESSMENT RESULTS

CHAPTER 11

What Doesn't Work?

I entitled this chapter "What Doesn't Work," but I want to make a disclaimer. I am not saying that you should not use any of the practices listed, as some may be out of your control, like home visits, which were required in my district for years, and homework may be mandated at your school site. However, I want you to look at each indicator and the profound preponderance of research that shows the practice does not give us the accelerated results we want for achievement. Some may come as a surprise, like homework and team teaching. I team-taught for many years and adored it. My students did very well academically and it worked because my team teacher and I had a common understanding of expectations. Others will come to you as no surprise, like summer vacation and retention. We all complain about the summer slide and have known for years that retention does not work as kids get older.

The goal behind this chapter is to shed some light on our practices and think about ways to start the conversation about what really works and what we might want to put on the back burner. Ok, let's get started!

Retention ○ Effect Size of -0.16

Retention is the practice of keeping students behind a grade level because they did not make adequate progress the previous academic year. Many schools promote these students socially as they get older because they do not want 16-year-olds in middle school. The social stigma of being retained also plays a huge role in defeating the student's confidence in their ability to learn. With a negative effect size of -0.16, the practice of retention appears to do more harm than good in the long run.

As a former kindergarten teacher, I can remember that many of my colleagues held students back or retained them because we thought that it would be easier for them socially. As kids get older, however, they are more aware and often feel othered when they are retained. I have talked to many students who have a great fear of being held back from their peers.

In many schools, we still see retention as a common practice in kindergarten through fourth grade. The practice is seen less as kids progress above the fourth grade. It is almost never practiced in middle school and high school. In fact, the exact opposite often occurs: I see a lot of kids socially promoted in middle school and high school because of their age and maturity level, rather than their skill level.

Research suggests that students who are retained are more likely to drop out of school. This is often due to the negative social stigma students face when they do not move ahead with their classmates.[7] Dropping out is also likely when students are older than their classmates and are teased for being retained.

There is no set formula used when retaining kids, but here are some of the most common steps taken when retention occurs.

---

7   A. Jacob, B. Lefgren, and National Bureau of Economic Research, *The effect of grade retention on high school completion,* Cambridge, MA: National Bureau of Economic Research, 2007.

1. Teachers identify students that seem to be having trouble with the content or who are developmentally delayed. Schools often have a mandatory screening document that is used to identify students who may need additional health, academic, or behavioral supports. Typically, this screen must be completed within 45 days of enrollment.

2. Once a need is identified, the school psychologist, administrator, and parent discuss an intervention plan.

3. After the intervention has been put in place for a designated amount of time, typically four to six weeks, the plan is revisited to determine how the student has progressed.

4. If progress is not seen after a few months of intervention, parents are notified that retention may be a possibility.

5. Most states require parent permission before retention can take place.

Case Study

Frank was much smaller than the other children in his grade and was the only child of a single mother. His mother, a high school graduate, held a job as a nurse assistant. Because Frank's mom was the only breadwinner for the family, she had to work double shifts, and Frank was left to be raised by his grandparents, who had no formal education. They did not read to him after school. Additionally, Frank had great difficulties paying attention in class. His mother was warned that he would be retained if he did not learn his alphabet. Frank's mom worked with him as best she could, but with her work schedule, it was very difficult. Frank was retained in kindergarten because he did not show any growth.

The following year, Frank made some progress and was promoted to first grade. However, because of his short attention span, Frank again began to struggle and his mom was warned again that he would be retained if he did not show growth. The cycle continued and Frank was again retained in first grade. Frank suffered from low self-esteem as the kids teased him for being retained twice in three years. He was much older than the other children, and he soon began to get into trouble. Frank dropped out of school when he was in the seventh grade to join a gang. He ended up in prison later in life, and he still cannot read. He relates this to being held back in school because he felt dumber than the other students and was only successful in getting into trouble.

✎ Reflection

Were you surprised that retention has a negative effect on student achievement?

_____

_____

_____

How does your school system feel about retention?

_____

_____

_____

Find a student who was retained in your school and talk to his current teacher about his progress. What did you find most interesting about how the student is progressing?

_____

_____

_____

Summer Vacation ☼ Effect Size of -0.09

Most schools in the United States have summer vacations for five to eight weeks during the summer months. There are some schools that have an extended school year, but students still often get at least a month or so off for summer vacation. Still, summer vacation has -0.09 negative effect on student achievement. Educators often talk about the summer slide or loss of knowledge students seem to exhibit when they return after summer break. Districts have tried to remedy this by holding summer school or having jump start programs where kids come back to school early. Even with all of our good intentions, the research shows that summer vacation places kids at a deficit.

One may argue that the -0.09 effect size does not outweigh the importance of giving teachers and students a break over the summer. As an educator, I can certainly attest to the importance of having time off to refresh. Many teachers pursue advanced degrees and work on educational projects over the summer. It is also a great time to reflect and make changes to the classroom for the next year. It may be beneficial for schools to think about ways to keep students engaged over the summer break so they don't fall back. Online learning opportunities or abbreviated school situations may be possible answers.

✎ Reflection

What are your thoughts on summer vacation?

_____

_____

_____

What are some ways to help students retain their learning during the summer while still giving them a necessary break?

_____

_____

_____

If you have ever taught summer school, how effective do you think it was for student academic growth?

_____

_____

_____

Multi-Grade/Age Classes
○ Effect Size of 0.04

Multi-grade/age classes, sometimes referred to as combination classes, group kids from different grade levels in one classroom. I was a student teacher in a third/fourth grade multi-grade/age classroom. I remember struggling to find resources to meet the standards for each grade level, which would let each of our students receive the education support they needed. This experience could relate to the low effect size. Students in combination classrooms do not learn any more or less than students in single grade classrooms.

The multi-grade/age classroom began in the one-room school house. Students aged five through twelve were grouped together in one room to learn the basics of reading, writing, and arithmetic. In the 1800s and early 1900s, this was the primary model of schooling in the United States and Europe.

The multi-grade/age class can be successful: I taught in this model as an experienced teacher, and our program ran well and our students progressed. My co-teacher and I, however, used response to intervention skillfully to ensure our students were getting what they needed to progress. Our Tier 1 instruction taught the standards and we grouped kids for Tier 2 and Tier 3 to provide extra support. We also were both master teachers with over 10 years' experience. With all of this in our favor, we had great success, but according to research, the typical combination class has only minimal academic success.

✎ Reflection

Would you like to teach in a multi-age/grade classroom?

_____

_____

_____

If you had the opportunity to teach in a multi-grade/age classroom, what do you think the challenges would be?

_____

_____

_____

If you taught in a multi-grade/age classroom, what do you think the plusses would be?

_____

_____

_____

What practices would you put into effect to ensure your multi-grade/age classroom was successful and showed more than nominal success?

_____

_____

_____

Mobility ☙ Effect Size of -0.34

It can be very detrimental to a student's growth when they move from school to school. Not only do they suffer from academic gaps from missing class and content and from not mastering specific standards, but it can also be psychologically and socially taxing for students to assimilate to another classroom. Students often suffer from stress and anxiety, which has been shown to be unfavorable to student achievement. Students learn better when they feel safe and secure.

Student movement from school to school has been a problem for years. Unfortunately, mobility is one of those things that we as educators don't have control over. Some districts have worked to streamline their central office processes so that kids with academic and social deficits can quickly be acclimated when they move to a new school within the district. This, however, is not so easy when children move from one district or state to another. I recently encountered a student who had moved from out of state and his Individualized Education Plan (IEP) for special education was not updated when he arrived at the new school. It took us a few weeks to realize we were looking at an older IEP and were not providing the necessary services the student needed.

The best response to the problem of mobility is to have a plan in place to assess kids immediately, and to obtain as much information about the learner as possible so proper placement and intervention or acceleration is implemented. Fill in information gaps by calling the child's previous school and talking with the child's parents. The school secretary can also help with finding the student's records, which can be very helpful in finding out more about the learner.

✎ Reflection

What steps does your district or school take to ensure students coming in later in the year are identified and receiving the services they need?

_____

_____

_____

What steps can you take to help ensure that students moving into your classroom are getting what they need academically?

_____

_____

_____

Write about a student who came into your room later in the year. How did you find out about the student as a learner?

_____

_____

_____

Mentoring ○ Effect Size of 0.15

Mentoring is a mutual relationship between two individuals to accomplish a desired goal. In education, mentors are used to nurture new teachers as they build their knowledge. Mentoring has an effect size of 0.15, which is not very impressive. However, many new teachers find mentoring to be very helpful in providing the moral support they need to embark on an educational journey.

Mentoring programs differ from district to district. Some mentoring programs have a clearly defined focus on teaching pedagogy and have a set curriculum that teachers follow. Other programs are more freeform, and mentors meet with their mentees infrequently. The level of interaction in the mentoring program certainly attributes to its effect size. The less time a mentor spends with their mentee and the less support they offer, the lower the effect size is likely to be.

As a new teacher I had a mentor who rarely, if ever, checked in with me. We had district trainings once a year that went over compliance and touched on instruction. I cannot say that my mentoring experience was rich or that it affected my ability to teach. I have, however, seen other mentoring programs where mentors are highly engaged with their mentees and provide targeted support. In these programs, you can witness more positive interactions and growth. The effect size of 0.15 reflects the minimal growth size, but when schools and districts apply systematic processes for their mentoring programs, increasingly positive effects are evident.

✎ Reflection

Describe the mentoring program at your school or district.

_____

_____

_____

What are some of the positive practices your mentoring program has?

_____

_____

_____

What would you suggest to make your mentoring program more effective?

_____

_____

_____

Teacher Subject Matter Knowledge
○ Effect Size of 0.09

This may come as a huge surprise for many, but teacher subject matter knowledge has an effect size of 0.09. According to research, a teacher may have a lot of knowledge about their subject, but that knowledge does not always transfer over into their teaching. Think about some of your college professors or high school teachers who knew their subjects in and out, but could not break the information down so that students could understand it.

It's true that strong content knowledge is important for teachers to have. In order to teach their subject, teachers need to have the confidence and knowledge to impart it to their students. After the Common Core Standards were adopted, many teachers indicated that the rigorous standards were more difficult to teach, so educational institutions have provided additional professional development opportunities to imbue teachers with the necessary content knowledge. Having this content knowledge helps teachers confidently teach the new standards.

However, knowing the content alone does not teach students. Teachers still have to use proven teaching strategies and best practices to ensure that students gain the knowledge necessary to succeed. That is what this 0.09 indicator implies: Simply knowing content does not ensure the knowledge will be transferred to students. It is only through skilled teaching that students learn.

✎ Reflection

Did this indicator's low effect size surprise you in any way?

_____

_____

_____

How does content knowledge help you teach your students?

_____

_____

_____

Why is content knowledge alone not enough to ensure student achievement?

_____

_____

_____

Whole Language ☼ Effect Size of 0.06

In the 1980s, whole language was viewed as the best way to teach students to learn to read. This reading methodology focuses on teaching students to learn to read by focusing on meaning and strategy over phonics. Students are taught to guess the meaning of a word they do not understand by replacing it with a word that makes sense and producing meaning. They learn to recognize core words and memorize them so they do not have to sound them out phonetically.

I taught during the height of the whole-language movement and saw the deficits this approach had. It was often difficult for students to memorize all of the words and to correctly come up with words that made a sentence meaningful. The phonics movement came to attention in the early 1990s, and teachers began providing more phonics instruction in the classroom. The reading wars became more prominent with the No Child Left Behind legislation.

Whole-language advocates hold the belief that as students see words in context as their teacher reads to them, they will soon memorize these words and be able to read them themselves. This might look like the teacher reading a Big Book with sight words. There is some truth to this method. As we see words repeatedly, we are more apt to recognize them and in turn memorize them. However, not every word can be memorized easily, and some students have a difficult time with comprehension.

The good thing about the whole-language model is that it encourages reading aloud, but the negative side is that it encourages students to read by sight, which is not a well-rounded strategy. When students learn phonics, they learn phonograms and their corresponding sounds, which provides a strategy they can use to read unknown words. Sight reading does not provide such an applicable strategy.

✎ Reflection

What are some benefits of using the whole-language method of teaching reading?

_____

_____

_____

What are the shortcomings of using the whole-language method of teaching reading?

_____

_____

_____

Write about your personal experience learning to read.

_____

_____

_____

What did you find most difficult in learning to read?

_____

_____

_____

How would a phonics or whole-language strategy have helped you with your struggles?

_____

_____

_____

Class Size ○ Effect Size of 0.21

I began my teaching career with over 30 kindergartners and no instructional assistant. It was exhausting, to say the least, but the kids did learn by the end of the year, which did not really support my perception that smaller classes equate to greater student learning. It turns out that smaller classes do matter in the primary grades K through 3. However, when we get to upper grades and high school, they really don't effect student learning outcomes.

Class size has been a focus in education for quite some time. Many districts around the United States have a cap of less than 25 for students in grades K

through 3. This is important, because educators in these grade levels have to differentiate instruction and work on teaching kids to read and master other skills in small groups. This is much harder to do when working with a class that has up to 30 kids. With classes that large, whole group instruction is mainly provided.

From the research, we find that class size does not adversely affect student achievement for students in middle school and above. Often, these grades can see class sizes up to 35 and teachers can still provide adequate instruction for peak student performance.

✎ Reflection

What was your initial thought when you saw the class size had a 0.21 positive effect size?

_____

_____

_____

Write about your experience teaching a smaller class versus a larger class. Did you find that you had more success with the smaller class?

_____

_____

_____

How can you make a larger class work so that student achievement continues to grow?

_____

_____

_____

Summer School ○ Effect Size of 0.23

Summer school has been around for many decades. I know that when I was a teacher, we had summer school almost every summer to help our struggling learners catch up. According to Hattie's research, summer school has an effect size of 0.23. You may ask, why would summer school have such a minor effect size? One of the reasons is that the curriculum used during summer school programs doesn't always align to the deficits of students. Most summer school programs have curriculum that is broad and does not target specific standards. Another reason is that summer school is often provided as an alternative to retention, meaning students come in with huge deficits that they are expected to overcome in a four- to six-week summer school program. This would certainly contribute to its low effect size.

Summer school that is targeted and provides practice on student deficit areas can help students improve in their learning. Most summer schools don't provide such experiences. Instead, they provide a more generic curriculum that touches on many standards. Since most students attending summer school have deficits to close, having a more structured, systematic approach to our summer school programs may help improve this practice. Some districts are looking into programs that are more targeted and direct so that summer school can be more conducive to student need.

✎ Reflection

Do you think summer school works? Why or why not?

_____

_____

_____

If you could design the perfect summer school, what would it entail?

_____

_____

_____

Write about a positive experience you had with summer school, either as a teacher or a student. What made this experience positive?

_____

_____

_____

Inquiry-Based Teaching
○ Effect Size of 0.31

Inquiry-based teaching involves posing questions or scenarios and allowing students to provide solutions. It may be surprising that inquiry-based teaching has an effect size of 0.31 because a lot of schools use this approach to support problem-based learning approaches. These are typically viewed as positive, productive ways for students to practice their problem-solving skills and prepare for jobs in engineering and science.

One of the problems with inquiry-based learning is that it has very loose rules for execution. If the teacher is unsure of exactly what students should take away from the lesson, inquiry-based learning can be a time waster that doesn't provide any formal, concrete learning.

As educators, we do want to expose our students to the problem-solving model and have them work independently to solve problems and come up with solutions. Though inquiry-based learning can help achieve this, its lower effect size of 0.31 can be attributed to programs without structure. Students need monitored, feedback-based systems to ensure they are adequately performing and progressing toward their chosen targets. Without this, students may be performing tasks inefficiently or incorrectly. This is why bringing in feedback (effect size of 0.75) and problem solving teaching (0.61) are so important.

✎ Reflection

Write about a time when you used inquiry-based teaching.

_____

_____

_____

What are the benefits of using inquiry-based teaching?

_____

_____

_____

How can you strengthen your inquiry-based teaching to make it more meaningful for students?

_____

_____

_____

Homework ○ Effect Size of 0.29

Homework and school are almost synonymous. Teachers have used homework for decades to have students practice what they are learning in school. Interestingly, Hattie's meta-analysis shows that homework has a mere 0.29 effect size. This has caused shockwaves through the education community.

I, for one, did my share of homework as a student, and I assigned homework as a teacher. Homework is just one of those things that is ingrained into the world of education. However, studies find that most of the time, students practice things incorrectly when they complete homework. This makes it even harder for the teacher to un-teach incorrect methodology and misconceptions. Another reason homework does not have a very high effect size is that parents are often unable to help children with their homework. This is especially the case when students move into higher grade levels and are presented with more complicated work.

Homework is a part of the framework of education in the United States. Teachers make homework folders and homework calendars that are skillfully designed to spiral through the essential skills of their given grade level. Each year, teachers start the school year by explaining how the homework folder works and what the expectations are for turning in assignments. I have sat through hours of open house nights where teachers have shared their expectations for homework with parents. With all of this time and effort, you would expect a more positive outcome than 0.29. The fact is homework does not render enough positive growth for all the effort many teachers are putting into it.

There are some things to keep in mind if your school requires homework. Have the students read books at their level for homework. This will serve as a great way for students to practice fluency and comprehension. You can also have students review work from the previous year or quarter to help them solidify skill in a particular subject. The key here is to make sure students are familiar and proficient with a standard or strategy before setting them loose to practice it on their own.

✎ Reflection

Is your homework routine working for you? Why or why not?

_____

_____

_____

How can you make your homework assignments more effective and ensure that students are practicing correctly?

_____

_____

_____

What are your thoughts on having your school stop giving out homework altogether? How popular do you think this decision would be?

_____

_____

_____

Home Visits ○ Effect Size of 0.29

Home visits were popular in the late '80s and early '90s. Educators were required to visit parents at the start of the school year to help them feel more welcome to the school. I liked the idea of going to visit parents in their homes and seeing where my students lived, but it took a lot of my planning time for the school year, and that was often the only time I saw many of my parents. With an effect size of only 0.29, home visits are not highly indicative of student achievement.

Home visits are not practiced as frequently as they used to be, but there are still some schools that require them. The purpose of home visits is to build community and to ensure all stakeholders are invited to the table. I like the idea of home visits when they have a structured purpose and plan. For instance, if a parent is unable to come to the school due to health reasons, a home visit would be appropriate to keep the parent from being isolated. In our high-tech world, home visits can now be conducted using technology. There are many applications that allow individuals to talk and see others at the same time. This might become the wave of the future in home visiting. Again, as with homework, the effort and time put into home visits does not necessarily equate to a tremendous amounts of success. Finding other ways to connect with parents may prove to be more effective.

✎ Reflection

Write about a time when you went on a home visit to a student's home.

_____

_____

_____

What are the pros and cons to home visits?

_____

_____

_____

What is an alternative to a home visit that you can conduct?

_____

_____

_____

CHAPTER 12

Next Steps

This book has been jam-packed with the different indicators that John Hattie's meta-analysis has shown to be correlated to positive student achievement and growth, as well as those that have been correlated with ineffective or minimal positive effect on student achievement. His research is powerful, because it allows us to really hone in on what works best in education.

Some of the positive practices noted should come to you as no surprise. I don't think anyone would be shocked to know that Response to Intervention has a positive effect on student learning (effect size of 1.07) or that giving feedback (0.75) is correlated with improving student achievement, and that both are used to support student growth and success. On the other hand, it may be surprising to learn practices that have strong roots in our educational system such as homework (0.29) and summer school (0.23) have lower effect sizes.

Where Do We Go from Here?

You may be wondering where to go from here. You have read about diverse learning practices and their effect sizes, both positive and negative. The job of an educator is to provide the most substantial educational experience as possible. This means that educators, as a group, are held to the expectation of providing fruitful, research-validated instruction.

You may be working in a system that still employs some ineffective practices. If this is the case, your next step is to get this research to the decision-makers in your school or school district and start the conversation so positive change can occur. You may ask, how would I do something like this? It can be intimidating to bring forth new information to your boss, especially if they have mandated the inefficient practices in your school or district. The best way to get the word out about a positive research practice is to read more about it yourself so you can come up with a strong argument for or against it. In the appendix, I have provided information about research articles, websites, and books that you will find useful as you embark on your self-study of what works best in schools according to educational research. This process of teacher collaboration, which we discussed in Chapter 3, will be most effective in your quest to impart positive change.

✎ Reflection

How will you start a conversation with your school leaders or team about reevaluating or changing your school pedagogy?

_____

_____

_____

What are your greatest reservations about bridging this conversation?

_____

_____

_____

What can you do to combat this fear and move forward?

_____

_____

_____

How can a growth mindset help you in your quest for change?

_____

_____

_____

Evaluate Your Current Practices

Take a week to evaluate the practices that you are currently using in your classroom and the practices that are prevalent in your school. Self-evaluation can be difficult because we have biased views of our own lives. We are often unaware of what we are doing because we are so busy with the act of doing. To evaluate yourself, you must step back for a while and assess yourself almost as an outsider looking in. Remember this is for your eyes only and holds no judgment about your abilities as a teacher. Ok, let's get started!

In order to self-assess, follow a prescribed system that will require that you look at your lesson plans and the systems you have in place in your classroom and on your campus/district. This task will take several days to a week to complete, because you want to ensure you are objective and that you have time to reflect. This assignment will only be successful if you really think about the practices that you most often utilize and note them.

▦ Procedure

1. Look through your lesson plans for the past month. Make a note of how often you teach in small groups versus whole groups.

2. Check out the walls in your classroom and make a note of the posters you have, the bulletin boards, and the classroom rules.

3. Look at your data. Use the accompanying chart to help you keep track.

Monthly Instructional Practices

Number of whole group lessons	
Number of small group lessons	
Number of lessons where you applied specific direct instructional practices	
Number of lessons where metacognition was utilized	
Number of opportunities for spaced practice	
Approximate number of classroom discussions in the month	
Number of times students worked collaboratively	
Total:	

After you tally the total for each of the seven concepts, use the following scale to rank your progress:

90–140: Great job! You are consistently employing best practices in instruction. Keep it up, and share what you are doing with your fellow teachers so they can benefit from your knowledge.

89–60: You are implementing best practices in most of your lessons. Find additional ways to incorporate these practices in your lessons so you can continue to impact student achievement. You are doing great!

59–30: You have created a foundation for using best practices in the classroom; a little under half of your lessons incorporate these high-impact strategies. Continue building on this foundation and aim to incorporate best practices in half of your lessons.

29–1: Make a plan to implement at least one of the high-leverage strategies in your lesson plans. Track your progress again after a month of incorporating them and view your results again.

0: Think about ways to begin providing more opportunities to use these high-leverage strategies in your class. Find a partner who may be interested in planning together to find ways to incorporate some, if not all, of these practices, in your lessons.

Evaluate Your Assessments

Review your assessment procedures from the past month. Consider graded materials, student conversations, and other assessment methods.

Notes on Monthly Assessments

MASTERY OF LEARNING	
SELF-REPORTED GRADES	
RESPONSE TO INTERVENTION	
FEEDBACK	
EARLY INTERVENTION	

Read all of your above comments and summarize them in 300 to 400 words. How are your assessment practices affecting student growth? What can you change? Reread your summary and internalize it as a way to voice your ideas about what works best in instruction and aids in student achievement.

Evaluate Your Management System

Use the following statements to evaluate your management system. Be sure to have a copy of your most recent student and/or parent handbook and a copy of your classroom rules or contract.

Are your rules written in positive terms?   Yes   No

Do you sometimes catch yourself labeling kids as smart, naughty, or challenging?	Yes	No
Do you have a quiet spot where kids can sit to cool down?	Yes	No
Have you drafted your classroom management plan?	Yes	No
Do you teach your kids how to behave inside and outside of the classroom?	Yes	No
Has your administrator ever complimented you on your well-managed classroom?	Yes	No

Review your responses to the above survey. Reflect on steps you will take to provide a more inclusive and direct management system to ensure students feel safe and secure in your classroom.

Evaluate Your School Systems

This evaluation allows you to look at the bigger picture of what is happening on your school site. As we have reiterated throughout the book, some things are out of your scope of control, but building awareness is the first step in stimulating change. Big things can happen when school systems develop sustainable, systematic changes. This assignment will be most helpful in bringing the conversation to the table.

What are three things outside of your control that you know are not best for kids and you wish you could change?

_____

_____

_____

What are two things you would change about your school management system?

_____

_____

_____

What two suggestions would you give your colleagues to ensure student home-work is meaningful, rather than an exercise in solidifying incorrect practices?

_____

_____

_____

What one thing would you change about your school's Response to Intervention program?

_____

_____

_____

If you could suggest an alternative to summer school, what one thing would you suggest?

_____

_____

_____

What alternative to retention might you suggest to your school administrator or fellow teachers who support retention practices?

_____

_____

_____

Read all of your above narratives and summarize them in 300 to 400 words. Afterward, reread your summary and internalize it as a way to voice your ideas about what works best in instruction and aids in student achievement. Use this as your springboard for bringing the conversation to light to help spark change.

_____

_____

_____

Conclusion

I hope this book has helped make Hattie's research more visible for you. Just as we try to ensure our students are clear about our teaching methods, I want to ensure you have a clear understanding of how the meta-analysis process occurred, and you can easily implement those high-leverage strategies in your own classroom and school. Please take the time to complete the exercises in each chapter. This will allow you to process the information and build a deeper understanding of the concepts so you can own them and confidently implement them.

Please contact me if you have any questions about any of the activities or information that is shared. It is my goal to lead this collective inquiry as we all work together to make impactful change in our schools for generations to come.

Appendix

Additional Resources

Visible Learning

Hattie, John. *Visible Learning: A Synthesis of Over 800 Meta-Analyses Relating to Achievement*. London: Routledge, 2010.

Hattie, John and Gregory C. R. Yates. *Visible Learning and the Science of How We Learn*. London: Routledge, 2013.

Waack, Sebastian. "Visible Learning." 2017. https://visible-learning.org.

Waack, Sebastian. "Visible Learning: Hattie's Rankings." 2017. https://visible-learning.org/nvd3/visualize/hattie-ranking-interactive-2009-2011-2015.html.

Growth Mindset

Brock, Annie and Heather Hundley. *The Growth Mindset Playbook: A Teacher's Guide to Promoting Student Success*. Berkeley, CA: Ulysses Press, 2017.

Dweck, Carol. *Mindset: The New Psychology of Success*. New York: Ballantine Books, 2006.

Dweck, Carol. "Carol Dweck Revisits the 'Growth Mindset.'" *Education Week*. September 22, 2015. https://www.edweek.org/ew/articles/2015/09/23/carol-dweck-revisits-the-growth-mindset.html.

Collaboration

Sawyer, Brook, and Sara Rimm-Kaufmann. "Teacher collaboration in the context of the responsive classroom approach." *Teachers and Teaching: Theory and Practice* 13 no. 3 (2007), pp. 211-245.

Friend, M. and L. Cook. *Interactions: Collaboration Skills for School Professionals*. White Plains, NY: Longman, 1996.

Goddard, Y. L., and R. D. Goddard. "A theoretical and empirical investigation of teacher collaboration for school improvement and student achievement in public elementary schools." *Teacher College Record*, 109, no. 4 (2007), pp. 877-896.

Graham, P. "Improving teacher effectiveness through structured collaboration: A case study of a professional learning community." *RMLE Online: Research in Middle Level Education*, 31, no. 1 (2007).

Reibman, S., L. Hansen, and A. Vickman. "Collaboration as an element of school culture: Biblioteca Las Americas." *Teacher Librarian*, 34 no. 2 (2006): 73-75.

Street, Hilary and Julie Temperley, eds. *Improving Schools Through Collaborative Enquiry*. London: Continuum International, 2005.

Teacher Clarity

Fendick, Frank. *The Correlation Between Teacher Clarity of Communication and Student Achievement Gain: A Meta-analysis*. University of Florida, 1990.

Wang, Weirong. "A Cross-Cultural Study of the Relationships Between Teacher Credibility, Teacher Clarity, and Nonverbal Immediacy." PhD diss., Illinois State University, 2007, ProQuest (ATT 3280914).

Parent Communication

Dyches, Tina Taylor, Nari Carter, and Mary Anne Prater. *A Teacher's Guide to Communicating with Parents: Practical Strategies for Developing Successful Relationships*. Upper Saddle River, NJ: Pearson Education, 2011.

Jones, D., G. Eaker, P. Keyserling, M. Taylor, J. Perks, National Association for the Education of Young Children, & South Carolina Educational Television Network. *Partnerships with parents*. Washington, DC: NAEYC, 1990.

Classroom Management

Cassetta, Gianna and Brook Sawyer. *Classroom Management Matters: The Social-Emotional Learning Approach Children Deserve*. London: Heinemann, 2015.

Hulac, David and Amy Briesch. *Evidence-Based Strategies for Effective Classroom Management*. New York: Guilford Press, 2017.

Literacy

Gambrell, Linda and Lesley Mandel Morrow, eds. *Best Practices in Literacy Instruction*. New York: Guilford Press, 2014.

National Reading Panel. "Teaching Children to Read: An Evidence-Based Assessment of the Scientific Research Literature on Reading and Its Implications for Reading Instruction." February, 2000. https://www.nichd.nih.gov/publications/pubs/nrp/Documents/report.pdf.

Mathematics

Clayton, Gypsy Abbott and the Educational Resources Information Center. *Effective Mathematics Teaching: Remediation Strategies: Grades K-5*. US Department of Education, 1987.

Iddins, C., T.R. Smith, and California. *Handbook for Planning an Effective Mathematics Program: Kindergarten through Grade Twelve*. Sacramento, CA: Department of Education, 1982.

Sullivan, Peter, Doug Clarke, and Barbara Clarke. *Teaching with Tasks for Effective Mathematics Learning*. New York: Springer, 2013.

Assessment and Grading

Canady, Robert Lynn, Carol Canady, and Anne Meek. *Beyond the Grade: Refining Practices That Boost Student Achievement*. Bloomington, IN: Solution Tree Press, 2017.

McKenna, Michael C. and Katherine A. Dougherty Stahl. *Assessment for Reading Instruction*. 2nd ed. New York: Guilford Press, 2008.

Reeves, Douglas. *Elements of Grading: A Guide To Effective Practice*. 2nd ed. Bloomington, IN: Solution Tree Press, 2016.

Hattie's Rankings

Use the following chart to easily compare the effect sizes of the different strategies discussed in this book. For a more complete visual aid, and for information on strategies not discussed in this book, visit https://visible-learning.org.

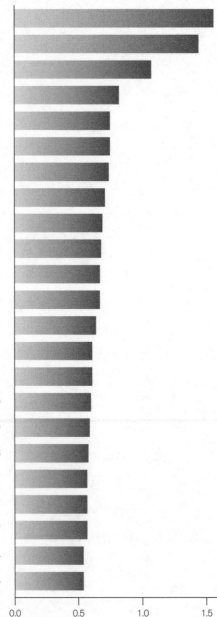

Strategy	Effect Size
Collaboration (Collective Teacher Efficacy)	1.56
Self-Reported Grades	1.44
Response to Intervention	1.07
Classroom Discussion	0.82
Teacher Clarity	0.75
Feedback	0.75
Reciprocal Teaching	0.74
Spaced Practice	0.71
Metacognitive Strategies	0.69
Classroom Behavior	0.68
Vocabulary Programs	0.67
Repeated Reading Programs	0.67
Self-Verbalization and Self-Questioning	0.64
Not Labeling Students	0.61
Problem Solving	0.61
Comprehension Programs	0.60
Direct Instruction	0.59
Mastery Learning	0.58
Home Environment	0.57
Socioeconomic Status	0.57
Worked Examples	0.57
Student-Centered Teaching	0.54
Phonics Instruction	0.54

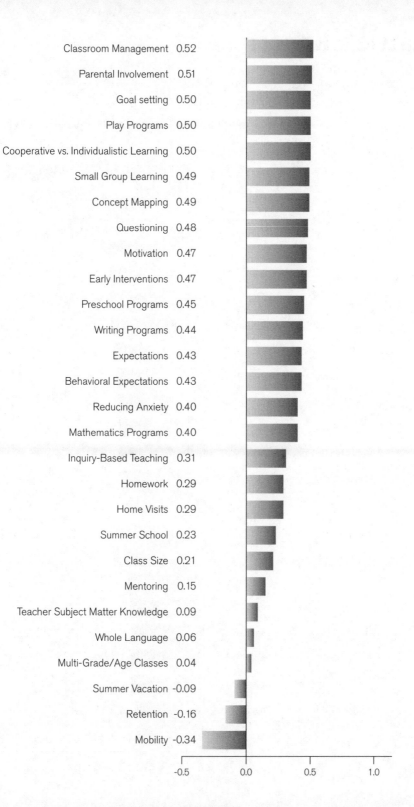

Classroom Management	0.52
Parental Involvement	0.51
Goal setting	0.50
Play Programs	0.50
Cooperative vs. Individualistic Learning	0.50
Small Group Learning	0.49
Concept Mapping	0.49
Questioning	0.48
Motivation	0.47
Early Interventions	0.47
Preschool Programs	0.45
Writing Programs	0.44
Expectations	0.43
Behavioral Expectations	0.43
Reducing Anxiety	0.40
Mathematics Programs	0.40
Inquiry-Based Teaching	0.31
Homework	0.29
Home Visits	0.29
Summer School	0.23
Class Size	0.21
Mentoring	0.15
Teacher Subject Matter Knowledge	0.09
Whole Language	0.06
Multi-Grade/Age Classes	0.04
Summer Vacation	-0.09
Retention	-0.16
Mobility	-0.34

-0.5   0.0   0.5   1.0

Acknowledgments

Thank you to Dr. John Hattie and your immense contribution to the field of education via your meta-analysis. Your work has truly helped bring the focus back to what works in schools. Without your dedication and hard work, this book would not have been possible.

Thank you to Ulysses Press and my exceptional editor Shayna Keyles for your tireless support and guidance as I worked on this book. You were motivating and helped ensure this book came to life, and that the ideas came across clearly and effectively.

Thank you to my colleague Elizabeth Patterson for your continued support as I wrote this book. Our early morning conversations were motivation to keep going. You are a blessing!

To my loving husband Chuck, thank you for your support and continued faith in me. You are my rock. My success can be attributed to your belief in me. Thank you!

To my dear son Caleb, you are my source of inspiration. Thanks for being such a kind and generous soul. You are destined for greatness!

To my father Virgil, thank you for always stressing the importance of education and always encouraging me to write my stories.

Finally, this book is dedicated to my dear, beloved mother Nevida. I miss you dearly but know you are always with me in spirit.

About the Author

Dr. Felicia Durden is an award-winning educator with over 20 years' experience in education. Felicia has taught all grade levels, from kindergarten through college. She deems herself a lifelong learner who strives to provide essential information for educators. Dr. Durden has served in many roles in education, including teacher, Title 1 specialist, district literacy administrator, college professor, and most recently, principal of a K–5 school in a large urban school district. Contact her at fdurden77@gmail.com or through her website, findingbalanceinlife.com.